T0286003

Beethoven in the Bunker

BEETHOVEN
IN THE BUNKER

Fred Brouwers

TRANSLATED FROM THE DUTCH BY

Eileen J. Stevens

Other Press
New York

Originally published in Dutch as *Beethoven in de bunker* in 2019 by EPO
Copyright © Fred Brouwers and EPO publishers vzw, 2019
English translation copyright © Eileen J. Stevens, 2022

FLANDERS LITERATURE This book was published with the support of
Flanders Literature (flandersliterature.be).

Unfortunately, the publisher has been unable to track down the copyright
holders for some of the illustrations in this book. Any persons or institutions
who would like to submit a claim are welcome to contact the publisher.

Production editor: Yvonne E. Cárdenas
Text designer: Julie Fry
This book was set in Legacy and Futura.

1st Printing

Library of Congress Cataloging-in-Publication Data
Names: Brouwers, Fred, 1948– author. | Stevens, Eileen J., translator.
Title: Beethoven in the bunker : musicians under the Nazi regime /
    Fred Brouwers ; translated from the Dutch by Eileen J. Stevens.
Other titles: Beethoven in de bunker. English
Description: New York : Other Press, 2023. | Includes bibliographical
    references.
Identifiers: LCCN 2022040712 (print) | LCCN 2022040713 (ebook) |
    ISBN 9781635423297 (hardcover) | ISBN 9781635423303 (ebook)
Subjects: LCSH: National socialism and music. | Music—Germany—
    20th century—History and criticism. | Music—Political aspects—
    Germany—History—20th century.
Classification: LCC ML275.5 .B7613 2023 (print) | LCC ML275.5 (ebook) |
    DDC 780.943/0904—dc23/eng/20220830
LC record available at https://lccn.loc.gov/2022040712
LC ebook record available at https://lccn.loc.gov/2022040713

Contents

Introduction
Music in the Bunker

In the late 1960s, including that magical year of 1968, I was a student of Germanic languages at the university in Leuven, the city where I was born. Student protests were raining down in Paris; in Leuven, there was a slight drizzle. As students, we rebelled against the blind authority imposed on us by our institution of higher learning, our parents, and the political establishment. Power for power's sake was thrown overboard and multiple political leanings were welcomed. This extended to the realm of my greatest passion, music. Various musical streams were mixed together. While marching in the streets, we sang "We Shall Overcome." Deep Purple played their *Concerto for Group and Orchestra* with the Royal Philharmonic Orchestra, conducted by Malcolm Arnold. I still get goosebumps thinking about Jon Lord's entrance on the organ! Classical composers like Cornelius Cardew and Frederic Rzewski wrote politically charged works. We embraced protest songs by Woody Guthrie, Pete Seeger, and Bob Dylan. Their European counterparts inspired us too, including Wolf Biermann in East Germany; Ewan McColl and Leon Rosselson in the United Kingdom; Boris Vian, Jean Ferrat, Georges Brassens in France; and our own Belgian Jacques Brel, who took aim at the bourgeoisie. We were familiar with bootleg tapes by the dissident Vladimir Vysotsky, which circulated clandestinely in the Soviet Union. Musicologists explained that Beethoven was both a musical genius and an enemy of dictatorial authority, as was clear from his Third Symphony. And hadn't Bach, the great master, been reprimanded during his years in Weimar for daring to clash with a student who happened to have wealthy parents? Pure class justice!

From the early 1970s on, I worked in the world of radio and television, and I carried the political sentiments of the 1960s with me. But let me be clear: the beauty and power of music and words always remained paramount. The connection with politics and the world at large was an extra dimension. My first project was a radio program entitled *Politheek*, a combination of *politics* and the Flemish word for "discotheque." Every week, I selected a political or social theme. I found an hour's worth of music to illustrate an endless stream of topics including sexism, homosexuality, racial discrimination, political dictatorship, slavery, the women's movement, anti-Semitism, and war. The music ranged from Bob Dylan's song about Rubin "Hurricane" Carter to Joseph Haydn's *Farewell*

Symphony. The 1970s were followed by decades of working on programs, both on radio and television, dedicated exclusively to classical music. Perhaps the best known of these is the Queen Elisabeth Competition, which I presented for thirty-five years. In 1983, Frederic Rzewski even wrote the required piece for that competition, although it was 100 percent music, unlike *The People United Shall Never Be Defeated*, a 1975 work in which the soloist was expected, among other things, to whistle and slam the piano lid.

My fascination for the connection between music and society never waned. In 2014, shortly after I retired, the city of Leuven commissioned me to organize a concert commemorating the start of the First World War. Leuven had been devastated by that conflict, becoming what is known as a "martyr city." It received attention and genuine support from the United States and the United Kingdom. For the memorial concert I chose the Mozart *Requiem* and a new work entitled *The Sack of Louvain*. Written by Belgian composer Piet Swerts, the work was based on four poems by war poets. The four vocalists chosen represented both reconciliation and the hope for peace: a Belgian tenor and soprano, Thomas Blondelle and Ilse Eerens; a German baritone, Dietrich Henschel; and an American mezzo-soprano, Vivica Genaux, all conducted by a British conductor, David Angus.

While working on that project, I often thought about the Second World War. It had ended in 1945, so 2020 was to be the seventy-fifth anniversary of the cessation of hostilities. Because of my background in media I always try to find ways of contributing to important historical landmarks. During my research, I stumbled across an article from August 2007 in the German magazine *Der Spiegel*. It was about the Russian invasion after the liberation and described the astonishing discovery made by a music-loving Russian soldier in Hitler's Berlin bunker: music written and performed by some very unexpected musicians. The idea for a book was born, focusing on the complex relationship between Hitler, the Nazis, and music.

After the Germans were defeated in 1945, a Russian military patrol led by Lev Besymenski searched Hitler's secret bunker in Berlin. There, various items were found (and greedily snapped up), but Besymenski, a music lover, focused on the record collection. Soldiers were grabbing jewelry, paintings, and other valuables, but he was content to take the gramophone records home with him. For many years, he never mentioned this unique collection to anyone. Instead, it's thought he played a few of the records for a couple of distinguished musicians. Emil Gilels was one: a pianist and the winner of the 1938 Queen Elisabeth Competition, known before the Second World War as the Eugène Ysaÿe Competition. The other was Kirill Kondrashin, the conductor.

When Besymenski died in 2007, his daughter Alexandra stumbled upon the remarkable record collection while clearing out her father's attic in the Russian village of Nikolina Gora. She mentioned her discovery to the German magazine *Der Spiegel*. A lot of people were keen to know which records the dictator had listened to. The resulting interview was revealing and raised a few eyebrows.

The inclusion in the collection of the *Flying Dutchman Overture* was no surprise. It's commonly accepted that Richard Wagner, although he'd been dead since 1883, was seen as the Nazis' composer-in-residence. In his operas Wagner delved into the Teutonic history of pure-blooded Germanic heroes. What's more, he wrote a book, *Das Judentum in der Musik* (usually translated as "Judaism in music"), bluntly asserting that Jewish people had poisoned the public's taste in the arts. This didn't hurt his reputation with the Nazis.

Ludwig van Beethoven was another composer seen as a German symbol. In the bunker, Besymenski found recordings of his Ninth Symphony and two piano sonatas, no. 24 in F-sharp and no. 27 in E Minor. The melodious and emotional accessibility of Sonata no. 24 was a good match with Hitler's tastes. Still, there were extra-musical aspects, as well. One of Beethoven's sayings was, "Strength is the morality of the man who stands out from the rest." Hitler could easily identify with such principles; he recognized something of himself in Beethoven, another man who had worked his way up from humble origins. That forged a bond. All the more surprising, then, that the performer on the recording was Artur Schnabel, a Jewish star pianist who had fled Germany in 1933. He had managed to escape, but sadly, his mother perished in the Theresienstadt Ghetto. In other words, while Hitler viewed Jewish people as subhuman *Untermenschen*, if they played enjoyable music he was prepared to look the other way. But, of course, that would have dented his credibility in the eyes of his supporters. This is why he kept the gramophone records carefully under lock and key. At least, until Besymenski stumbled across them.

Hitler was a great lover of opera. It's said that when he lived in Vienna, he attended a performance every day. Wagner is obviously one of the composers he admired — but the Russian Modest Mussorgsky? Mussorgsky was another *Untermensch*. Yet one of Hitler's favorite excerpts was the "Death of Boris Godunov," a dramatic scene from the opera of the same name. The version found in the bunker could hardly have been more Russian, with the bass Feodor Chaliapin singing the lead. Peter Tchaikovsky, thought to have been homosexual, was also one of Hitler's companions in the shelter. Tchaikovsky's famous Violin Concerto was in the drawer, performed by Bronisław Huberman (I'm starting to sound like a broken record), a Polish Jew who fled Europe in 1937. It turns out Huberman was notable for more than simply "being Jewish." He actively opposed Nazism and wrote a letter to several key German intellectuals and artists asking them to stand up to the regime. He was officially declared a "public enemy of the Third Reich."

Hitler's List of Five Records

Anton Bruckner rounds out the top three favorite Germanic composers, alongside Wagner and Beethoven. It didn't hurt that he was both a follower and loyal admirer of Wagner. But Bruckner also had something in common with Hitler. Like Beethoven, his background was humble, and yet he reached great heights. This forged another bond. After the announcement of the Führer's death on 1 May 1945, the Reichsrundfunk (or public radio) played the *Adagio* from Bruckner's Seventh Symphony, presumably from the 1942 recording conducted by Wilhelm Furtwängler. It was no coincidence that Hitler had chosen that music himself. He had always compared that symphony with Beethoven's Ninth. Bruckner had written the slow movement—which features instruments known as Wagner tubas—a few weeks before Richard Wagner died. So there's that symbolic connection again: Beethoven-Wagner-Bruckner: perfect background music for Hitler's death.

The Russian patrol also found several banned Jewish composers: the long-dead Felix Mendelssohn and Jacques Offenbach, and many "despicable" Russians, including Sergei Rachmaninoff and Alexander Borodin. These composers cheered Hitler's spirits in his Berlin bunker. He'd made a list of five records that were to be taken with him — at any cost — if he suddenly was suddenly forced to flee, which proves that he'd given the matter considerable thought. Included on the list were the Beethoven piano sonatas, the *Flying Dutchman Overture*, the Russian arias with Chaliapin, Tchaikovsky's Violin Concerto, and last but not least, Mozart's Piano Sonata no. 8 in A Minor, performed by none other than Artur Schnabel. When referring to the Nazis' preferred music in general and the choice of Mozart in particular, Robert Stolz, an immensely popular composer of operettas and light classics who had emigrated to the United States, once made a brilliant remark during a radio program: "It seems as if the Nazis put a steel helmet on Mozart, girded Schubert with a saber, and wrapped barbed wire around Johann Strauss's neck."

Hitler had fallen under the spell of the music and the talent of particular performers to such an extent that he forgot they were the enemy. This has led some historians to suggest he was not such a bad fellow, really. In this, however, they are overlooking the death toll weighing heavily on his conscience. While Hitler sat secretly enjoying previously recorded forbidden music in his bunker, musicians made of flesh and blood were denied a means of making a living. They died in concentration camps or in other war-related circumstances. Or they survived but ended up in psychiatric care; they managed to flee just in time; they sided with the regime, out of conviction or coercion; or they joined the resistance. All of which makes this an extraordinarily fascinating chapter in music history.

Readers curious to hear the works mentioned in this book should refer to the YouTube playlist detailed on pages 250–61.

Paul Abraham
The Would-Be Hollywood Star

In the 1940s and 1950s (and even into the 1960s), many Europeans grew up listening to radio broadcasts of songs such as "Ja so ein Mädel," "Yokohama Mama," "Pardon, Madame," "Toujours l'amour," and the unforgettable "Reich mir zum Abschied noch einmal die Hände." All these numbers are from operettas. As often happens with such arias, they went on to lead a life of their own. The artist who created these songs played the sad lead in what could have been the libretto of a tragic opera.

Instead, it was a brutal reality for the once celebrated composer Paul Abraham. He was born in 1892 in Apatin, a pleasant village along the Danube in what is now Serbia. He was Jewish and an ethnic Hungarian whose real name was Pál Ábrahám. The region then belonged to the extensive Hapsburg Empire. Little is known of Abraham's childhood; his public life began in 1910 when he left for the bustling cultural metropolis of Budapest. Many German speakers lived there, and as in so many

places in the Austro-Hungarian Empire, German culture was predominant.

Abraham became a student at the Franz Liszt Academy of Music. There, during his formative years, he composed a "Hungarian Serenade" for chamber orchestra, a concerto for cello and orchestra, and a string quartet. He later claimed he'd been commissioned by the symphony orchestra of Budapest to write the concerto. And that Eugene Ormandy, who later became a world-famous conductor, had played first fiddle when his string quartet was premiered. Neither of those claims can be verified. It's not clear if he wrote his second string quartet as a graduation project for his doctorate; he enjoyed bandying that title about, but in reality it seems he never graduated. Was he already showing a touch of his subsequent delusions of grandeur?

We know that he was active as a conductor of liturgical music for a time. He rounded off his first creative period in 1917 with a small-scale opera called *Etelkas Herz*, composed for a marionette theater. Although not entirely unsuccessful, he quickly realized that no pot of gold awaited him in the classical sector. And wouldn't you know, enormous riches just happened to be one of his fixations! Which explains why, for a decade or so, he delved into the world of business. Or, more specifically, playing the stock market. He may have inherited business acumen from his father, although Abraham's adventures in trading also ended in a minor key, with bankruptcy and a stint in prison.

In 1927 he again turned his attention to music. He got a job as kapellmeister — one could say "chief conductor" — at the Metropolitan Operetta Theater in Budapest. To supplement his income, he played the piano in coffeehouses and some newly emerging jazz clubs, which brought him into contact with "light" or popular music. When he contributed four numbers to the operetta *Zenebona*, a collaborative work, he was struck by listeners' positive response to his songs. It quickly dawned on him that he might have a future in popular music. He packaged his "change of heart" in a nice anecdote. He said he once heard a hit song by Pasquale Perris, "Ich küsse Ihre Hand, Madame," the title melody from a film of the same name, starring Marlene Dietrich. When the saleswoman told him that a million and a half copies of the number had been sold, he was sold as well, and he began writing popular music to beat the band. And although his first complete operetta wasn't a great success, it did contain one song — "Der Gatte des Fräuleins" — that brought him fame in Germany.

As a result, he was commissioned in 1929 to write the music for the film *Melodie des Herzens*, which became hugely popular. The following year brought another triumph with his third operetta, *Viktoria*. He outgrew Budapest and moved to Berlin, a city that had wrested the title of "operetta capital" from Vienna *Viktoria,* during its German premiere in Leipzig, was renamed *Viktoria und ihr Husar (Victoria and Her Hussar).* It was a smash hit and, with that operetta alone, he earned the equivalent of one and a half million euros. The story had been written by two of the greatest opera librettists of the time, Alfred Grünwald and Fritz Löhner-Beda (there is a chapter devoted to Löhner-Beda later in this book).

Jazz Mixed with Operetta

One of the reasons for Abraham's success was his introduction of a completely new sound. He added lighter jazz influences and contemporary dance rhythms to the oh-so-typical classical operetta idiom in the tradition of Offenbach-Strauss and Lehár. This was a golden combination. After only a few months, he became incredibly wealthy, and *Viktoria* was followed by one success after another. *Die Blume von Hawaii* was his next hit. Followed by *Ball im Savoy,* which premiered on 23 December 1932, just as the curtain was closing on the Weimar Republic. It was an unprecedented success, but it was to be his last hit at the box office. He had rocketed to great heights in all of Europe. But his career was destined to be brief. Thanks to record sales, fees, and copyrights, he had acquired vast wealth. The money did not make him happy. He held lavish parties in his chic Berlin mansion almost every day; his goulash fests for the neighbors were legendary.

The troubles began during the filming of *Ball im Savoy*. He was attacked and roughed up by fascist extras. The *Schauspielhaus* then barred him from attending his own film. Gradually, it all became too much for him. He vented his frustration in his work as a composer and orchestra leader, and in bars, casinos, and various sexual escapades. The film was still playing in theaters when Hitler assumed power from German chancellor Kurt von Schleicher on 30 January 1933. In March and April of that year, the filmed version of *Blume von Hawaii* was slated for release in German movie theaters. But that soon changed. Everything Abraham had created was quickly placed on the Nazis' index of banned artworks, and his entire fortune was confiscated. High time, in other words, for him to retreat to Budapest with his wife.

A credible story about the episode has been confirmed by numerous Abraham researchers. Apparently, upon leaving Berlin, he handed the key to his safe to his butler/chauffeur. It contained his compositions, which he planned to further develop and market in better times. Unfortunately, things didn't turn out as planned: his "confidant" pilfered the manuscripts and sold them to erstwhile composers who happened to be Aryan. They went on to make a big splash with the numbers — without, of course, disclosing their source.

Abraham continued to work for a few more years, writing for films and the stage in Hungary and Vienna. In Budapest, he produced a sports operetta, with which he thumbed his nose in a musical sense at Germany. *Roxy und ihr Wunderteam* was to be his final European operetta. The off-the-wall work, which had its premiere in December 1936, initially revolved around the Hungarian water polo team: the choice of subject was no coincidence. During the Berlin Olympics in 1936, the Hungarian team had won the gold medal, beating the Aryan "wonder team." When Abraham subsequently moved to Vienna, the operetta was reworked. In the Theater an der Wien, it was the Austrian soccer team who took center stage. And again, this was no accident. On 24 May 1931 the team handed Germany a resounding defeat: 6-0. Although *Roxy* achieved mild success, Abraham's Berlin salad days were over forever.

In 1939 after the Anschluss, when Vienna was no longer safe for Abraham, he left for Paris. He stayed there for about a year. In émigré circles, he met Yvonne Louise Ulrich. She later became the wife of the Nazis' fanatical adversary Robert Stolz. After Paris, Abraham went to Casablanca, where he earned a living as a bar pianist. He did the same at his next destination: Cuba. From there, via Miami, he ended up in New York. When he arrived in the United States he was penniless. A friend, his compatriot Alexander Paal, a Hollywood movie photographer and producer, had paid Abraham's required five-hundred-dollar entrance fee. Abraham was convinced that the Americans, and certainly Broadway, would fall for his compositions, but his music failed to catch on. The Americans didn't care for his concept of jazz. They felt, by the way, that jazz and operetta didn't belong in the same genre.

Destitute and Delusional

Abraham didn't have much success as a pianist. His royalties had been frozen in Germany, so he descended into financial ruin and became mentally unhinged. With that, the first symptoms of syphilis appeared, a catastrophic combination, which led to his complete collapse. A series of fantastic stories followed. Unfortunately, they were fantastic in the literal sense of the word. He started telling people he had been asked to write the music for influential Hollywood films. This wasn't true.

Another time — according to Robert Stolz — Abraham invited dozens of friends to his wedding to Hollywood star Ilona Massey. Invitations were sent out for the massive reception to be held in the luxurious Hotel St. Moritz. But when the guests arrived with flowers and presents, there was no bride to be seen. Abraham couldn't remember anything about a wedding. Back at his hotel, he demanded that the elevator boy take him up to the seventeenth floor forty-two times, shouting "faster, faster" each time.

In the end, he was committed to the Creedmoor Psychiatric Center in Queens. He'd been standing on a conductor's podium in the middle of New York City's busiest intersection, dressed in rags—but wearing white gloves—conducting an imaginary orchestra. He remained at Creedmoor until 1956, helping in the kitchen and doing various odd jobs, including sweeping the stairs. Any one of these episodes could have been a scene from some madcap operetta.

His visitor's visa had long since expired. Still, he was allowed to remain because the hospital fees were covered by his royalties, which had gradually been unfrozen. Back in Germany, Alexander Paal set up an Abraham Committee; the public had utterly forgotten him. In 1956 he was repatriated to Germany with several other war victims. He lived for another four years. He was— ironically enough—first treated at the University Medical Center Hamburg-Eppendorf by Dr. Hans Bürger-Prinz. That man had been a member of the Nazi Party and had participated in numerous Nazi organizations. He had a brown-shirted past. As a legal expert, he decided on the forced sterilization of individuals considered genetically ill. It was only years later that Bürger-Prinz's war crimes were fully exposed.

Following Abraham's release, he and his wife, Charlotte, who had arrived from Hungary, moved into an apartment in Hamburg. By then, the issue with the frozen copyright royalties had been entirely resolved. He also received a healthy monthly allowance from the German nation. In 1960, Paul Abraham died of cancer. To his last breath, he believed he was still living in New York City. He regularly reported on the Broadway premiere of his masterful operettas in letters to friends.

Arturo Toscanini
The Tyrant

It was a primary school teacher who discovered the enormous musicality of a little boy named Arturo, born in Parma in 1867. Thanks to the intervention of that schoolmaster, Toscanini later became a maestro himself, although in a different branch: he grew to become one of the most iconic conductors of the late nineteenth and early twentieth centuries. For many, he was the greatest conductor of his era, sensational as the artistic director of La Scala in Milan, the Metropolitan Opera in New York, and the New York Philharmonic Orchestra. He also led the NBC Symphony Orchestra, which a few wealthy Americans had set up especially for him.

His debut as a conductor was unexpected, making it all the more spectacular. He had been the principal cellist of a touring opera company when, during a performance in Rio de Janeiro, the audience booed the conductor out of the orchestra pit. The small, shrewd Italian leaped onto the conductor's podium, urged on by his colleagues, who were well aware of his phenomenal

memory. He then conducted Giuseppe Verdi's *Aida*, from the overture to the final chord, entirely from memory. He had never before led an orchestra. That same night, the opera company's board made him the artistic leader for the rest of the season. During the weeks that followed, he conducted twelve different operas in a total of twenty-six performances, all without a score. It was the stunning launch of a monumental international career. He was one of the handful of classical musicians who have the charisma and moral authority to compete with sports heroes, rock stars, and world leaders. Just as rare: he also became the prototype of artists who used their immense popularity to fight injustice and dictatorship.

"Mussolini, the King-Emperor, the Pope? Swine! All of them!"

Toscanini's birth coincided more or less with the unification of Italy. His parents embraced that development, allowing him to bask in the Italian spirit throughout his childhood. Although he grew up in what was then a new country, there were still a few thorny issues, including the regions of Trento and Trieste. To him, they were undeniably part of Italy. And so, at the beginning of the First World War, he advocated showing strong resistance toward German-speaking forces. Toscanini canceled his well-paid engagements and conducted nothing but benefit concerts. The money raised was earmarked for out-of-work musicians, and he went so far as to sell his own home. In 1917 he put together an army orchestra and headed for the front. He conducted his orchestra on Monte Santo while the Italians were trying to wrestle another mountain out of the Austrians' control, less than a mile away. When shots were exchanged during the performance, he refused to stop, and for this he received a medal.

When the war was over, the Italian government showed little ability to bring order to the country's chaos. Therefore it's no surprise that Toscanini, like many others, saw salvation in the person of Benito Mussolini, whom he had heard speak during a meeting in Milan. Mussolini presented himself as a figure of strength, and at that time, he still had a communist agenda. He was just as disillusioned as Toscanini about the injustices incurred by Italy from the postwar settlements, and about the country's lack of decisiveness. In 1919 Toscanini was even listed as a candidate for the elections. But neither he nor Mussolini got enough votes. With that, Toscanini's career in party politics came to an end. Needless to say, Mussolini's career did not.

Toscanini's next politically artistic act was to establish a new orchestra, which later became the orchestra of the recently reorganized La Scala. He performed with that orchestra in Rijeka in present-day Croatia, to demonstrate that Istria was also part of Italy. The invitation had come from the soldier and writer Gabriele D'Annunzio, who had led the brief occupation of the city in 1919–1920. Rijeka, also known as Fiume (Italian for "river"), is an important port. It became a point of contention during negotiations after the First World War, although Italy certainly had a historical claim. Moreover, the vast majority of the city's population was Italian.

Toscanini's nationalism survived undaunted, but his sympathy for Mussolini—who by then had resorted to violence and tyrannical behavior—did not. Toscanini's initial admiration turned to hatred, as is clear from one of his many quotes: "If I were capable of killing a man, I would kill Mussolini." In December 1922 he had his first run-in with the new leaders who had recently come to power. At a performance of *Falstaff*—the Verdi opera with which La Scala was reopened after the First World War—a group of fascists raucously demanded he perform their party hymn, "Giovinezza." Toscanini refused. As he was about to give the opera's downbeat, the tumult grew. He snapped his baton in two and stormed out of the orchestra pit, cursing and shouting. Only when, during intermission, a member of management told the audience that "Giovinezza" would be sung and played following the performance, was Toscanini prepared to continue with the opera's ending. When the opera was over, the same manager tried to order the opera company to sing the hymn — with piano accompaniment — but a seething Toscanini intervened. "They are not going to sing a damned thing!" and "La Scala artists aren't vaudeville singers!" He capped it off by ordering everyone back to the dressing rooms. In the end, the pianist played that "damned thing" entirely on his own.

Toscanini won that battle, and he later managed to prevent the fascists from gaining control of the board of directors of La Scala. He also refused to display the obligatory public portrait of Mussolini, so there wasn't one in La Scala. There was a significant battle surrounding the posthumous premiere of Giacomo Puccini's opera *Turandot*. Il Duce dearly wanted to attend the premiere, but he insisted that "Giovinezza" be played beforehand. Toscanini answered that, in that case, they would have to find another conductor for "Giovinezza"...and for *Turandot*. The chief conductor won that round from Il Duce, who diplomatically stayed home for the premiere.

The tug-of-war ceased in 1928 when Toscanini left La Scala to take command of the New York Philharmonic. He made one more hugely successful tour with La Scala in Germany and Austria. In 1930 he toured Italy with his new American orchestra, causing another upheaval. The royal family attended the concert in Turin, meaning that the national anthem had to be played before the concert, followed by "Giovinezza." Toscanini also took a dim view of the monarchy. And I quote: "Mussolini, the King-Emperor, the Pope? Swine! All of them!" He was prepared to play the first piece — the national anthem — but under no circumstances would he conduct the second. A solution was soon found: a military band took the stage as soon as the American orchestra was seated. They played both hymns and then disappeared.

Mussolini paid spies to follow the conductor and find ways to push him around. When Toscanini was in Berlin and invited to Fascist Party receptions, he always answered that he was too tired to attend. If they insisted, he didn't mince words. He said it wasn't because he was tired but because he was an anti-fascist who thought Mussolini was a tyrant and Italy's oppressor. He would rather forsake Italy than give up his convictions. Mussolini read that statement, and in 1931, when the maestro was in Bologna to conduct a concert in honor of composer Giuseppe Martucci, thugs from the party beat up Toscanini and his wife. The concert was canceled, and the furious audience charged the streets. Reactions and responses piled up, making life miserable for Toscanini, but he did not bow to pressure. His passport was confiscated, heralding many years of exile. Toscanini didn't return to Italy until 1946 for the inaugural concert in the restored La Scala: his La Scala.

The Conductor Who Held His Ground

Toscanini's opposition to fascism went beyond the Italian borders and made full use of his artistic weight and charisma. The Italian regime didn't dare try and stand in his way. And so, in the early 1930s, he conducted at the Wagner Festival in Bayreuth—he was so honored he refused all payment. The tenor Lauritz Melchior remembered the exacting chief conductor weeping the first time he set foot in that bewitching theater. After Hitler assumed power, Toscanini sent him a telegram condemning his racist politics and boycott of Jewish musicians. Hitler answered within two days, sending a personal request for the *Hochverehrter Meister* to return to Bayreuth. Toscanini flatly refused: "I must fight for musicians who are persecuted by the Nazis." Richard Strauss took over for him. No wonder, then, that one of Toscanini's most famous quotes concerns his colleague: "To Strauss the composer I take off my hat; to Strauss the man, I put it back on again."

However, Toscanini had no problem conducting the Vienna Philharmonic, both in Vienna and at the Salzburg Festival, where he felt he could relax. But this was in 1937. In February 1938, when the Austrian chancellor Von Schuschnigg visited Hitler in Berchtesgaden, he made some concessions to the Nazi regime. For Toscanini, a line had been crossed. He sent a telegram from

New York, saying, "I must withdraw my collaboration because of a change in the situation."

Toscanini earned both praise and hate mail as a result, but he clung firmly to his convictions. He had judged the situation correctly: German troops were welcomed into Austria with open arms just one month later. Toscanini's principles also kept him from conducting in Russia, both in the time of the tsars and during the Lenin and Stalin eras. He expressed his views by avoiding specific places and by visiting others. In 1936, for instance, he traveled at his own expense to Palestine to conduct a new orchestra there for free. The orchestra—which would later become the Israel Philharmonic—was an initiative of the Jewish violinist Bronisław Huberman.

After Toscanini had refused his engagement in Salzburg, the mayor of the Swiss city of Lucerne invited him to conduct there instead. This signaled the start of what, to this day, is one of the world's most important music festivals. The story goes that approximately one-third of the audience members were Italians who had crossed the border specifically to attend those concerts. A member of the secret police reported, "I do not believe all those tickets were bought for the love of art."

In April 1954, at the age of eighty-six, the maestro, who had for his entire life conducted everything from memory, lost control. He had a memory lapse, put his hand over his eyes, dropped his baton, and left the stage. He never conducted in public again. However, he subsequently corrected some recordings with which he hadn't been satisfied. At his death in 1957 in New York, he entered the annals of history as a symbol of freedom and humanity. And yet, his tale has a few bitter footnotes. Toscanini was able to determine the sound of an entire orchestra and interpret the score. He did that with his gestures, aura, and by becoming one with the music. But it turns out that Toscanini was also a member of the generation that behaved tyrannically toward orchestras. Just picture it: a small angry man on a rostrum stamping his foot, swearing, throwing scores, kicking the piano, snatching the bow from a violinist's hands, breaking his baton in two, tearing his jacket in search of a handkerchief, spraying saliva while bellowing. He had acquired enough power to do so. However, he exercised his authority in the service of art and not to fulfill sadist motives. Thanks to him, the opera, which had been dominated by expensive and capricious singers, was modernized. He was able to focus on the music and the power of the story. His motto was: Everything for the composers and their work. But he did have enemies, who reproached him not only for his attitude toward orchestral musicians but also for his technical limitations and distaste for modernism.

Yet Toscanini continued unabated. In his skirmishes with colleagues, he pulled out all the stops to maintain his exalted position. He ensured that potential competitors were not invited to conduct at the opera houses where he was the artistic leader. He also used his press contacts to guarantee glowing reviews. Some critics even put him on a par with Beethoven. Competition and even battles between musical stars have been around since the dawn of time. Between that and his often troubled love life (including numerous affairs with such celebrities as Geraldine Farrar, Lotte Lehmann, and Rosina Storchio, to the despair of his ever-faithful wife), there is ample material for another book.

Richard Strauss
The Opportunist

Toscanini tipped his hat to Strauss the musician, but he kept it firmly on for Strauss the man. Which is to say, he found Strauss a great composer but a small human being. In all likelihood, this had nothing to do with Strauss's striving for personal fame. Toscanini was no stranger to that himself. But it did reflect Strauss's position during the Hitler era. Wasn't Strauss for a time the chairman of the Reichsmusikkammer (Reich Chamber of Music), the Nazi institution charged with promoting "good German music" by Aryan composers? Hadn't he behaved in a manner that was detrimental to Jewish colleagues? And didn't he dedicate one of his most touching lieder — "Das Bächlein" (The brooklet) — to Goebbels? And what about his statement that German music, from Mozart by way of Beethoven and Schubert to Wagner (and by extension, to Strauss), represented the pinnacle of humanity's cultural development? Why was he friendly with the questionable conductor Willem Mengelberg, even dedicating his *Heldenleben* to him?

And is his *Metamorphosen* for strings indeed a monument to all the war dead, or is it simply a lament following the destruction of such sacred German cultural institutions as the Semperoper in Dresden or the Goethe House in Frankfurt? Is there sufficient evidence to label him an evil Nazi, or are matters in fact less black-and-white?

Strauss was born in Munich in 1864, the son of Franz Strauss, a horn player in the Bavarian court orchestra. His mother, Josephine Pschorr, was from a prosperous brewer's family. Young Richard studied philosophy, aesthetics, and art history at the University of Munich. He combined his studies with thorough musical training, including piano, violin, composition, instrumentation, music theory, and untold hours of practice. By all accounts he began composing at the age of six. When he was sixteen, his First Symphony was conducted in Munich by Hermann Levi (what's in a name)? His Second Symphony was presented in New York when he was barely twenty. Strauss also furthered his reputation as a conductor.

He quickly became one of the most influential musicians of his time, maintaining that position until his death in 1949. Initially, Strauss held Wagner in high esteem, along with Mendelssohn and Mozart. But in time he leaned toward modernism. During that period, Strauss flirted with atonality, a type of music lacking traditional relationships between the keys, in which every note functions independently. Unfortunately, atonal music does not offer the average listener much to hold on to. In Germany at the time Strauss was counted among the inaccessible experimentalists. However, he only strayed briefly, perhaps because he realized he risked alienating the general public with such music. In fact, had he pursued atonality, he would likely have been relegated to the *Entartete* (or degenerate artists) list. He soon returned to the traditional fold.

A cursory glance at his achievements before his appointment to the Reich Chamber of Music in 1933 speaks volumes. He had worked as a conductor in Bayreuth, was Royal Kapellmeister in Weimar, conducted the Munich Opera, led the Vienna Philharmonic, and was appointed general music director of the Berlin opera and as head of the Vienna State Opera. And that's just the start. Between engagements, he traveled around the world as a guest conductor. He paid frequent visits to Belgium, conducting a series of popular concerts in the Munt Opera House in Brussels. Strauss was also a guest of the Antwerp Society for New Concerts, founded by Lodewijk Mortelmans and Lodewijk De Vocht. They also hosted Gustav Mahler, Sergei Prokofiev, and Igor Stravinsky. In 1906 and 1907 Strauss conducted the Kursaal Orchestra in Ostend, Belgium. In Amsterdam, Strauss regularly worked with Willem Mengelberg's Concertgebouw Orchestra.

On the composing front, he created such orchestral works as *Aus Italien* (*From Italy*), *Also Sprach Zarathustra* (*Thus Spoke Zarathustra*), *Don Juan, Don Quixote,* the *Symphonia Domestica, Eine Alpensinfonie* (*An Alpine Symphony*), and outright brilliant art songs of which "Zueignung" ("Devotion") and "Morgen!" ("Tomorrow!") are just two examples. His achievements in opera included *Elektra, Salome, Der Rosenkavalier, Intermezzo,* and more. At the time, Strauss would have been a welcome addition in any regime in the world to their equivalent of the Reich Chamber of Music.

One could hardly consider the young Strauss an objectionable and fervent National Socialist. He had one guiding principle throughout his entire career: he sympathized with any regime that promoted his music. What's more, he didn't hide his blatant opportunism. Strauss had served the German kaiser and the Austrian emperor. He was highly regarded in the German-Austrian Republic, so it is no surprise that he managed to get along with "the present lot" as well. All that mattered was his success. The man who was such a genius that he claimed he "could set a telephone book to music" just couldn't be bothered with politics.

And yet, in the 1920s, Strauss did tilt to the right. When journalist Samuel Wilder—no one less than film legend Billy Wilder—asked him in 1925 about Mussolini, Strauss expressed admiration for the Italian fascist leader. In fact, Strauss was to meet Mussolini on several occasions. He apparently confessed to his half-Jewish librettist, Hugo von Hofmannsthal, that he could see the advantages of a dictatorship. However, he was not particularly enthusiastic about the figure of Hitler. By 1932, Strauss thought Hitler had had his day.

Yet later, Strauss was rather pleased with the new chancellor: at last, here was a politician who was exceptionally interested in culture (meaning music, Strauss's music). The two spoke for the first time in 1933 in Bayreuth, where Strauss filled in for Arturo Toscanini. The latter had boycotted the Nazi regime. In Bayreuth, Strauss and the Führer are reported to have discussed musical issues, specifically a reorganization of the musical system. This seems plausible; few genuinely Nazi statements can be attributed to Strauss. Nevertheless, he viewed Hitler as a man who could help him achieve such dreams as overhauling the copyright system to protect classical composers' rights and reforming the German opera houses.

Hitler and Goebbels, for their part, recognized that, in the realm of culture, "their" musicians were their most important export products — even eclipsing their writers. Warm feelings were beside the point. Incidentally, Goebbels considered Strauss a "decadent neurotic." Strauss noted in his diary that he thought Goebbels's Jew-baiting was a "disgrace to German honor." Hitler was a genuine admirer of Strauss's music—but not of Strauss, the person. During Hitler's Vienna period, when, aged seventeen, he was "something of a bum," the future führer managed to scrape together enough money to attend the premiere of Strauss's *Salome*. There he sat, like a pauper among the crowned heads. It is worth noting that *Salome* is the story of a Jewish historical figure, and its tonality is considerably dissonant. It is also based on the work of that "degenerate," Oscar Wilde. Hitler's early exposure to Strauss helps explain Strauss's appointment to the Reich Chamber of Music, which regulated all the country's musical activity. While other musicians of stature had graciously declined the honor, Strauss accepted the position. Maybe it would further his success.

Is It Hats On or Off to Richard Strauss?

There are doubtless plenty of arguments for coming to Strauss's defense. For example, he and Wilhelm Furtwängler were invited by Hitler and Goebbels to represent Germany as cultural figureheads at the 1937 Paris World's Fair, where the two most important German chief conductors were slated to conduct. Furtwängler accepted the invitation but then "forgot" to make the Nazi salute. Strauss said he was "sick," a diplomatic form of protest. When his fellow conductor the Jewish Bruno

Walter fell out of favor, and Strauss was asked to take his place for a few concerts at the Gewandhaus in Leipzig, he initially demurred. It was only after the intervention of a Jewish impresario and at Walter's own insistence that Strauss acquiesced. And while he did compose a hymn for the Olympic games in Berlin, he later clarified in a letter to a friend that he considered the "honorable" commission distasteful. He never agreed with the exclusion of Jewish people from musical life.

The ban on performing the works of such Jewish composers as Felix Mendelssohn was something Strauss would never understand. What's more, by discreetly cooperating with the regime, he was able to help a few people. (This was, incidentally, the case with many musicians who, after the war, were all too easily accused of collaboration.)

It began with Strauss's own family. His only son, Franz, was married to a Jewish woman, Alice Grab, the daughter of a Czech textile industrialist. Alice quickly became Strauss's favorite daughter-in-law and an invaluable secretary. He never ceased showering her with compliments. Because of her background, Strauss feared that his beloved grandsons, Richard and Christian, would be expelled from school as "not pure" and subjected to untold horrors. When their grandmother and a few members of Alice's family were arrested, Strauss wrote to the authorities. When this failed to produce the desired result, he had his chauffeur drive him to There-sienstadt so he could plead in person for their release. Once there, he announced himself as "Richard Strauss, the composer of *Der Rosenkavalier.*" It was to no avail, but his efforts placed him in a vulnerable position vis-à-vis the authorities.

The strongest argument for understanding Strauss's position comes from the writer Stefan Zweig. In his book, *The World of Yesterday: Memories of a European,* Zweig, who later took his own life out of sheer disillusionment as a victim of anti-Semitism, described in his characteristically mild and objective manner how Strauss continued to offer help during those trying times. And I, for one, have complete faith in Zweig. After the death of Hugo von Hofmannsthal, the librettist of the greatest number and most successful of Strauss's operas, the composer asked Zweig to be his collaborator. Zweig had previously written texts for other musicians, but he was deeply honored by the recognition of someone of Strauss's caliber. Their first joint project became *Die schweigsame Frau,* based on Ben Jonson's *The Silent Woman.* A few weeks after Hitler came to power in January 1933, when the opera was almost finished (if only in its piano version), German theaters were banned from performing the work of non-Aryans. The prohibition extended to pieces in which a Jewish person had made even a negligible contribution. As a result, Zweig had expected Strauss to call an immediate halt to their partnership. But nothing could have been further from the truth: Strauss reported calmly and with no innuendo that he had begun work on the opera's instrumentation. Moreover, Strauss was eager to get started on another opera with Zweig. He added that no one could tell him to dissolve the partnership. The Jewish contribution to *Die schweigsame Frau* was sizable, including input from the librettist, the publisher, and the man who wrote the piano arrangement. Zweig emphasized that Strauss had always been fair and friendly toward him and had never turned his back or displayed the slightest hint of anti-Semitism. Strauss's attitude is best summed up by this quote from his letter addressed to Zweig: "Do you believe I am ever, in any of my actions, guided by the thought that I am 'German'? I recognize only two types of people: those who have talent and those who have none. 'The people' do not exist for me until they become the 'audience.'"

That is Strauss through and through. Strauss's Jewish coworkers were briefly spared precisely because the Nazis could not afford to sever their contacts with such a well-known composer. The respite was temporary, however, because the Nazi Party was always searching for a new club with which to beat the "Jewish cur." The premiere of *Die schweigsame Frau* forced the party to choose: whether to go against their musical figurehead and ban the performance or not. The gravity of the matter is clear from the fact that Hitler himself read Zweig's libretto to see if he could find grounds for condemning the opera. He found nothing, and in the end Strauss got his way. The opera was staged, "contrary to all the laws of the new German Reich."

Shelter from the Storm

After the second performance, however, the times caught up with them. The opera was banned in Dresden and in all of Germany. And there was more news: Richard Strauss had resigned as a president of the Reich Chamber of Music. Why? A letter Strauss had written to Zweig had fallen into the hands of the Gestapo. In it, he implored the author to start work on their new opera as soon as possible. He also openly expressed his personal unease with the whole situation. Strauss had no option but to resign. With that, *Die schweigsame Frau* was truly silenced.

Strauss withdrew from public view, and for most of the war he sheltered in Vienna. Then, in 1945, he moved to Switzerland. Finally, after his denazification in 1948, he returned home to Garmisch-Partenkirchen, Germany. There he spent the rest of his days with his lifelong spouse, soprano Pauline de Ahna, in the idyllic estate built with royalties from his opera *Salome*. One day after the war, an American soldier named John de Lancie, who had participated in the liberation, visited Strauss. De Lancie was a professional oboist with the Pittsburgh Symphony Orchestra. He asked if Strauss had ever considered writing an oboe concerto. The reply was a curt *Nein*, but the idea took hold.

Some months later, de Lancie read in the newspaper that Strauss had composed an oboe concerto at the request of an American soldier. It was a classical work that clearly reflected the spirit of Mozart, whom Strauss had idolized in his youth. The oboe concerto was to be one of Strauss's final masterpieces. The first recording of the piece was made in 1948 by Léon Goossens, an Englishman with Flemish roots. There's little doubt that Strauss preferred fulfilling an American's request for an oboe concerto to composing an Olympic hymn for Hitler. Strauss seems nowhere as happy and pleasantly smiling as in his photograph with John de Lancie. If someone's life concludes with a song cycle like *Vier Letzte Lieder* (*Four Last Songs*), much can be forgiven.

Elly Ney
The Fervent Anti-Semite

To Hitler and his followers, Beethoven was a musical hero. That's why it's no coincidence — and certainly no wonder — that pianist Elly Ney adored the great master. Musicians who sympathized with the Nazi regime had primarily opportunistic motives. They simply wanted to carry on with their careers in their own countries, or they hoped to elbow their way to the international top. In both cases there was usually little in the way of explicit political posturing or activities. However, some musicians were more enthusiastic about paying lip service than others. They were rewarded for their loyalty and support for the regime. A few were elevated to a status far beyond their true artistic merit. Many years after the fact, it remains difficult to sort out which of those opportunists belongs in heaven, hell, or purgatory. But there were undoubtedly some who had decidedly fascist and anti-Semitic ideas, and the pianist Elly Ney (b. 1882 in Düsseldorf) is clearly a member of that camp. She may have been doubly predisposed: her mother was a music

teacher, and her father was a militaristic and xenophobic platoon sergeant. At the time of Ney's death in 1968, she lived in Tutzing, an idyllic spot on the Starnberger See in Upper Bavaria. Some years earlier, the local authorities had made her an honorary citizen. But shortly after her death, she was stripped of that title. The great lady had also been honored with a bronze bust on the Brahmspromenade: Brahms, another of her favorite composers, had once spent four summers resting and writing music in Tutzing. When the German Christlich-Soziale Union in Bayern (Christian Social Union in Bavaria) or CSU party lost its absolute majority in the 2008 elections, a left-leaning political wind blew through the village. The new mayor, a political independent named Stephan Wanner, immediately had the portraits of both Ney and one of her chamber music partners, cellist Ludwig Hoelscher, removed from the *Rathaus*. The municipal council decided not to take down the statue on the Brahmspromenade but a different memorial text was added:

> The famous pianist and Beethoven interpreter Elly Ney lived in Tutzing from 1937 and was one of the founders of the Tutzinger Musiktage [Tutzing Music Days]. However, she was a vocal supporter of National Socialism, a fervid anti-Semite, and she enjoyed the protection of the

National Socialists [Nazis]. In 2009, the municipality distanced itself from her anti-Semitic remarks and her National Socialist convictions. It condemns all forms of anti-Semitism, racism, and hatred. The purpose of this plaque is to keep history from fading from memory, and to serve as a warning against profiting from, or being duped by, systems of totalitarianism.

Following her musical training in Cologne and Vienna, Ney became an outstanding pianist. After her first solo recital in 1904, she quickly rose to fame in Germany. But she wasn't just after her own glory. You could say she was on a mission for classical music in general and the works of Beethoven in particular. She didn't restrict her appearances to the grand concert stage and performed with equal zeal in schools, universities, hospitals, factories, and prisons. She believed that everyone was entitled to the arts.

Well, not precisely "everyone," as we shall see. In 1911 Ney married the Dutch violinist Willem van Hoogstraten. Considering Elly's blind devotion to Beethoven, there was only one possible name for their daughter, born in 1918: Eleonore. When Beethoven was still a teenager living in Bonn, his first love was Eleonore von Breuning, to whom he later dedicated a few compositions. Leonore is also the name of the female lead in his only opera, *Fidelio*.

In 1914 Ney formed a piano trio with her husband and a cellist. She appeared with that ensemble on the most glamorous of German and European stages, or as a soloist with the best orchestras. Her reputation ensured that she, together with the conductor Wilhelm Furtwängler, was among the few European musicians invited to the United States after the First World War to help get the recording industry off the ground. She traveled to the States in 1921. For her first concert in Carnegie Hall, she played an all-Beethoven program, as one might expect.

She remained active in the States until 1930, with great success. Her concerts received wide acclaim, and the recordings she made for the Brunswick label doubled the company's sales. Her husband primarily worked on his conducting career. It was a turbulent period in their private life, and the couple divorced. Ney then briefly married an American, Paul Allais, who was active in the coal sector. It appears she had simply been "on a break" from her marriage to Willem van Hoogstraten, however, because she soon reunited with him. They never remarried, but they remained together for the rest of their days. When she returned to her *Heimat* (homeland) in 1930, she struggled to regain her German citizenship, because her marriage to an American "enemy"—she hadn't divorced Allais—meant she was no longer German. She had to prove that her return would be a boon to German society. And her status as a famous pianist smoothed the way.

And so, our story gradually approaches the year 1933. Ney displayed great admiration for Hitler from the start. In that year she wrote a letter to Willem: "I just heard Hitler speak for forty-five minutes. I was deeply moved. Enormous strength. Read his speech. This is truth spoken from a deeply sensitive and fervent human spirit. He spoke to me from the soul about art. Finally, it is being said out loud, and the way is clear."

The Reich's Piano Großmutter

It soon became plain which "way" she was referring to. She actively began spreading the Nazi word and supporting Hitler's ideology. There was an unmistakable signal as early as 1933, when the *Berufsverbot* (professional disqualification) meant a replacement had to be found for her colleague, the equally famous Rudolf Serkin, for a performance in Hamburg. Ney refused to fill in, because she could not bear to perform in place of a Jew.

Ney quickly joined various organizations, including the Bund Deutscher Mädel (League of German Girls). That was just one of many youth organizations inspired by Hitler, this one targeted at girls and young women. They were taught party doctrine, they collected money and clothing, and when things turned desperate toward the end of the war, they even took part in military maneuvers. Ney became a sort of mother figure to the group, and this fed her vanity.

She gave lectures placing Ludwig van Beethoven and north European music within the Nazi context, asserting that music written by the northern composers was without doubt superior. She was convinced that only someone with a Germanic soul could interpret Beethoven correctly. This ruled out the Jewish competition. It certainly didn't hurt that she was a Beethoven specialist. Nazis from every sector—political, economic, military, and cultural—all suffered from an advanced form of Beethoven mania. No wonder. Like Hitler and the entire Nazi movement, Beethoven stood for struggle and ultimate victory.

When the Nuremberg Racial Laws banned Jewish musicians from performing Beethoven's music, Ney no longer had any rivals. She contributed to the 1936 Olympic games, receiving a commemorative medal from Hitler for her performance. In April 1837 she was granted the title "Professor." To show her appreciation, Ney joined the Nazi Party ten days later, becoming number 6,088,559. In 1939 she was appointed a senior professor of piano at the glorious Mozarteum in Salzburg. Like other musicians who sympathized with the Nazis, she was given a top position at the Mozarteum. Such jobs had previously gone to talented Jewish musicians or to opposition members who had either fled or been "eliminated." She supported Hitler's firing of Jewish people from essential posts. The story goes that, in Salzburg, she gave the bust of Beethoven a Hitler salute every time she walked past.

Throughout the war she continued to support the party in her own special way. In 1940 she was sent to the Netherlands to give some concerts. Once there, she complained about her accommodation in a letter to the minister of propaganda: "Staying in the Hotel Central is not very pleasant for me. I sincerely hope that no more Jews will be staying here, as they have in the past."

In 1941 she played a recital in Kraków for the NSDAP (the Nazi Party) in the General Governorate for the Occupied Polish Territories. It was but one of many concerts she gave throughout the war for the Nazi Party. Some concerts were held in military field hospitals. For her service, Hitler awarded her a War Merit Cross Second Class. She was referred to as "Hitler's pianist," although some staff members maintained he didn't enjoy hearing her play. There are, in fact, witnesses from that period who claim that, following her first sensational years on stage, Ney never quite reached the same technical heights again. Be that as it may, she more than lived up to her reputation. She wrote admiring letters to *Mein Führer.* On stage, she regularly read Hitler's writings aloud. On the night of 14 November 1940, Ney, also known as the official Reich's Piano *Großmutter*, received perhaps her greatest accolade.

The Reich's radio service broadcast Ludwig van Beethoven's *Moonlight Sonata*, with Elly Ney at the keyboard, just as the Luftwaffe's bombers were headed for Coventry to reduce that British city to rubble. The bombing raid's code name was Operation Moonlight Sonata. Although she may not have been aware of it at the time, that broadcast connected all the dots: the Third Reich, Beethoven, Hitler, Ney, and victory over the rest of the world.

In 1942 she again left no doubt as to her stance, even surpassing the great leaders. The occasion was a performance in Görlitz of Carl Orff's *Carmina Burana*. This composition was popular in the Third Reich. But for Ney, the work's rousing rhythms, bawdy texts, and abrupt shifts were much too modern. Elly Ney was visiting the city for a concert. She was in the audience, sitting next to the local leader of the Nazi Party. After the first few measures, she leaped to her feet and bellowed: "Cultural disgrace!" The party official followed suit, and they stormed out of the auditorium in a huff. Ney also had strong opinions about Stefan Zweig, Richard Strauss's librettist, calling him "ugly" and "Jewish-demonic." And she was firmly opposed to jazz. She thought it was dangerous music because of its "impure racial elements."

For Ney, the icing on the cake came in 1944 when she was placed on the *Gottbegnadeten Liste* (God-gifted list), put together by the German Ministry of Public Enlightenment and Propaganda, with a little bit of help from Goebbels and Hitler. The list included those who were great, *unersetzlich* (indispensable), and thus chosen by God. This exempted them from military service. As the end of the war approached, more and more artists were enlisted to fight—it was all hands on deck. The list contained names of more than one thousand artists, including conductors such as Karl Böhm, Eugen Jochum, Herbert von Karajan, Hans Knappertsbusch, and Clemens Krauss. Pianists included Walter Gieseking, Wilhelm Kempff, Elly Ney, and…Carl Orff. Let's just hope his name wasn't next to hers.

For the rest of her life, she refused to renounce Nazi ideology. For this reason, her favorite city of Bonn—Beethoven's birthplace—banned her forever from performing there. She challenged that decision, but in 1952 her appeal was turned down. Nevertheless, she continued to perform in other cities with some success. Outside of Bonn, in Bad Godesberg, she gave a recital in 1965, and the standing ovation lasted twenty minutes. The audience chose to appreciate Hitler's piano grandmother for her playing rather than condemn her for her behavior during the war.

Another talented pianist was Karlrobert Kreiten. He was somewhat younger than Ney and also hailed from Bonn. He kept an open mind toward all good composers, including *Untermenschen*. He remained openly critical of the Nazis' warmongering. After the defeat at Stalingrad, one of his neighbors overheard him saying that the Germans had lost the war, and she tipped off the Gestapo. He was arrested, tried, and, in 1943, executed by hanging in Berlin's Plötzensee Prison. Wilhelm Furtwängler's attempts to save him were in vain. Two capable pianists, but their lives couldn't have been more different. Music does not always by definition improve a person's moral fiber.

Josef Bor and Rafael Schächter
Two Camp Mates

Richard Strauss had asked his driver to take him to the Theresienstadt Ghetto to plead for the release of his Jewish daughter-in-law's relatives. Terezín (as it is now known) is a small city in the Czech Republic north of Prague, on the banks of the river Eger. The city's history is relatively brief because the Austrian emperor Joseph II founded it in 1780 and named it Theresienstadt in honor of his mother, Maria Theresia. It is a fortified city similar in style to the traditional French fortifications of Vauban. Although it had been a popular vacation destination for the Czech nobility, its primary importance was military. During the First World War, it served as a prison. Gavrilo Princip, the assassin of Archduke Franz Ferdinand of Austria, was held there for a time.

During the Second World War the Nazis continued the city's penitentiary tradition. At first the Gestapo used the bastion for political prisoners. But soon it became a transit camp for Jewish people destined for the gas chambers of Auschwitz. Initially, Jewish people from

Czechoslovakia were held there. They were later joined by prisoners from Austria, Germany, Denmark, and the Netherlands. Although it was not a death camp, the closing tally revealed that 33,000 people died in the ghetto itself. They primarily succumbed to overcrowding, its associated diseases, and poor nutrition. Approximately 88,000 people had been transported from Terezín to the gas chambers of Auschwitz and Treblinka. When the camp was liberated by the American army in 1945, there were precisely 17,247 survivors. Some 150,000 Jewish people had passed through the camp.

A Model City for the Jewish Population?

Rather cynically, the Germans used the small city as a propaganda tool. They didn't call it a "Preferential Camp" for nothing. In German, it was a *Vorzugslager*, with *Vorzug* meaning something like preference, advantage, or priority. The Nazis made sure that the city could look impeccable when it mattered. After a thorough *Stadtverschönerung* (civic beautification), it became a nicely maintained place with pleasant squares and parks, a hospital, a *Caféhaus* (coffeehouse) where someone with a special pass could while away a few hours to the sounds of forbidden swing music. There were shops, a church, a genuine concert hall, and good-looking, well-groomed Jewish prisoners. And so when an international delegation from the Red Cross came to carry out an inspection, the Nazis managed, on two separate occasions, to pull the wool over their eyes. After a lightning-quick but thorough "scene change," they hoped to convince the delegation — and the rest of the world — that Terezín was a model city for its Jewish inhabitants.

A large percentage of residents were well educated: industrialists, intellectuals, and artists from various disciplines. Some were even renowned. Among the musicians were the conductor Karel Ančerl (who later became world famous) and the composers Pavel Haas, Gideon Klein, Hans Krasa, and Viktor Ullmann. After some initial resistance from camp leaders, the musicians were permitted to possess musical instruments and go about their business. No surprise that, in time, the musical life in Terezín rivaled that of an ordinary medium-sized city. For the Nazis, these musical activities contributed to the image of a Jewish model city. The artists were happy they were allowed to get on with their lives. The best were housed in the *Freizeitgestaltung* (leisure activities) division. They had protected status and better living conditions and were even exempt from deportation. Many of those who survived later testified they hadn't realized they were being used as pawns. Being so engrossed in music blinded them to the reality around them. One could almost call it a win-win situation — were it not that, when the time came, someone had to foot the bill.

I stumbled upon this beautifully disguised horror by accident. I visited Prague in the 1970s, where I bought a small book by an unfamiliar author, Josef Bor. It was titled, *Theresienstädter Requiem*, and had been published in the Deutsche Demokratischen Republik (DDR) by Der Morgen. There's also an English edition, titled *The Terezín Requiem*. Bor was the pen name of Josef Bondy, who was a Czech lawyer and author. He had lived in the camp, having arrived there in 1942 after an attack on a high-ranking Nazi named Reinhard Heydrich. Two Czechs, apparently coached by the British, had opened fire on Heydrich and thrown a bomb at his car. He was fatally injured and died later in the hospital. Heydrich's nicknames, "the Butcher of Prague" and the "Blond Beast," speak volumes. As a reprisal after his death, the village of Lidice was decimated. Masses of residents were captured and deported. The Czech composer Bohuslav Martinu later wrote an orchestral work called *Memorial to Lidice* to honor the city and its victims. In Terezín, Josef Bor narrowly escaped death. He took part in Terezín's *Todesmarsch* to Buchenwald in January 1945, when the Americans intervened just in the nick of time. They saved him, but the Americans arrived too late for the rest of his family.

One of Bor's camp friends was Rafael Schächter, a pianist and conductor. Schächter was born in Brăila, Romania, and grew up in Brno. He completed his musical studies in Prague, where he began his professional career. He was not a conductor on Arturo Toscanini's or Willem Mengelberg's level. His name cannot usually be found in encyclopedias of music or other reference books. He was limited to provincial performances. For a time, he was the conductor in an avant-garde theater. Then, in 1937, he founded an ensemble, Komori, to play baroque music, which was relatively unknown at the time. In this he was a trailblazer, because interest in the baroque era of music history was almost nonexistent. When in 1939 the Germans partially annexed the Czech Republic, renaming it the Protectorate of Bohemia and Moravia, Schächter lost his job because he was Jewish. He was banned from performing in public.

On 30 November 1941, he arrived in Terezín with Transport H, registration number 128. There, he set about staging opera performances almost immediately. Of course, there were plenty of professional musicians and some decent amateurs among those highly educated people. In the summer of 1942 he presented a production of Bedrich Smetana's *Bartered Bride*. It was so successful it ran for thirty-five performances. He accompanied the singers himself on a baby grand piano. Later, a thirteen-year-old girl who attended the opera wrote about it in her diary. She'd previously heard the work in Prague three times but said those performances couldn't hold a candle to the one in the camp. The next opera was *The Kiss*, also by Smetana. Then, September 1943 arrived.

A Requiem for a Divided Italy?

Josef Bor writes that Schächter had decided to perform Giuseppe Verdi's *Requiem*. That great work, and its cryptic symbolic texts, would ensure an artistic event capable of thumbing its nose at German tyranny. The Nazi leaders in the audience would have the "Dies Irae" flung in their faces. Its message: The day of judgment is coming for all who enslave, belittle, rape, rob, and murder. In the "Tuba Mirum," all must stand before the judge. They would not escape because everything is described in the "Liber Scriptus." God intends to punish the culprits, and the closing "Libera Me" is a cry for liberation. There was nothing misguided or far-fetched in Schächter's — or rather, Bor's — reasoning.

On the contrary: Verdi himself was not particularly well disposed to the Roman Catholic Church. In fact, he was rather anticlerical. Therefore, his *Requiem* was not intended for the church but for concert halls and even perhaps for the streets. Moreover, Verdi dedicated his requiem to the Italian author Alessandro Manzoni, a literary figure and a champion of the Risorgimento: the liberation of large tracts of Italian territory from domination under all sorts of foreign powers, and the subsequent unification of the country. Verdi's "Libera me" can easily be viewed in a political light. It could even refer to the liberation of the good and the punishment of evil during the Last Judgment and the resurrection of Italy.

Schächter got to work, but he had to try and find four singers for those demanding solo parts! He managed to find them in Theresienstadt, of all places, along with a large choir. In Bor's book, the performance was accompanied by a full symphony orchestra. He describes how they managed to get ahold of all the instruments. A regulation stipulated that Jewish people outside the ghetto could not own musical instruments; they had to be surrendered to the government. In the ghetto, however, musical instruments were permitted.

In his telling, Bor had the instruments smuggled into the ghetto in various ingenious ways. First, a cello was carted in, hidden in a hay wagon. Then, Bor had the prisoners accidentally discover an entire arsenal of wind instruments in a bricked-up room left behind by a previous military unit. Finally, three double basses were driven into the camp on a cart filled with confiscated bric-a-brac under the very eyes of a naïve SS (*Schutzstaffel*) driver.

However...Bor's book is a work of fiction. The reality was less picturesque but no less heroic. Schächter did manage to drum up the solo singers and the 150-voice choir. But of course, an orchestra was out of the question. The performance was accompanied by two pianos. One had been brought in by the *Judenälteste*, a council of elders who served as intermediaries between the prison commanders and the prisoners. The other had been made available to the *Caféhaus* by the camp commandant. In Bor's novel, Rafael Schächter is one of the only characters using his real name. The others are difficult to connect with existing people, except for one man: a beggar who wanders around the camp, mockingly known as "Hofrat." On closer inspection, he proves to be an authority on music. As it turns out, this character is based on Kurt Otto Singer, the artistic director of the Berlin Kroll Opera. He was the founder of the crucial Jüdischer Kulturbund (Jewish Cultural Federation, originally called the Cultural Federation of German Jews, until Nazi authorities forced the organization to remove "German"). Also known as the Kubu, it was established in 1933 to support countless unemployed Jewish performing artists. The association had some 70,000 members, although other sources claim membership topped 180,000-plus. The Nazis tolerated the Kubu because it helped make the *Berufsverbote* seem like an enemy fabrication. Singer had gone to the United States to teach at Harvard shortly before the outbreak of the war. Following Kristallnacht, people urged him to stay in Boston, but he felt morally obligated to return to Germany. He died in January 1944 in Theresienstadt.

Rehearsing for the *Requiem* was touch and go. As one would expect, people regularly dropped out due to illness or death. Still, it was possible to hold the project together, partly because of the protected status of the performers. There were many rehearsals, first in a cellar, then in a large room that the commandant had made available. The performance was a success. Bor wasn't gilding the lily when he writes that, after the final chord, a deafening silence was broken by thunderous applause. But as stated earlier: someone had to foot the bill. Following the performance, almost the entire cast was transported to Auschwitz. Schächter had to put together a new choir. New prisoners were arriving continually. After the second production of the *Requiem*, they too were marched onto a train.

In December, the conductor started rehearsing for the next series of performances: third time lucky? He had to make do with a smaller choral ensemble, but he rolled up his sleeves and conducted no less than fifteen performances. In October 1944, the SS instructed Schächter to present an extraordinary concert. A delegation from the Red Cross was planning to visit the facilities in the company of Adolf Eichmann and several leading SS officers. The camp's "scenery department" again set to work. In no time, the hospital was brutally evacuated and transformed into a theater with a stage, curtain, and club chairs for the invited guests. Following the performance of Verdi's *Requiem*, there was a dinner for the honored guests. Eichmann found it hilarious that those Jews had been singing their own requiem. Hilarious to some. The entire cast—including Rafael Schächter—was sent on a death march to Auschwitz. Schächter arrived there on 16 October 1944 as number 943. For him, the Americans arrived too late.

Igor Stravinsky
The Man Who Adored Mussolini

Igor Stravinsky started to compose music for his *Mass* in 1944. At more or less the same time, the performers of Verdi's *Requiem* were being led to slaughter in Auschwitz. In Los Angeles, Stravinsky wrote a mass, nothing more. Apparently, he felt an "inner need." But did he love his neighbor as much as he loved himself, as the Christian faith teaches its followers? And what was his attitude toward his fellow humans in the years preceding and during the war?

"I am opposed to the right, abhor the left, and am altogether out of sympathy with the center."

"Stravinsky hated the Nazis!" states a sentence fragment taken from the writings of the American music publicist, conductor, and musicologist Robert Craft. He is referring among other things to a scrapbook kept by the maestro containing images of Göring and Himmler in compromising positions. But this can scarcely be taken

as proof: it could just as well be a form of humor. Especially considering that the same author writes elsewhere that Stravinsky, with "his pathological need for order," tended to feel at home with oligarchs and autocrats. And yet one also reads that the composer's anti-Semitism was lifelong and undying. Craft was undoubtedly in the know; he and Stravinsky were very close. They met in 1948 and became good friends. By that time, most of Stravinsky's most important works had already been written.

Stravinsky's breakthrough had come when Sergei Diaghilev, the Russian impresario best known for the Ballets Russes, presented *The Firebird*. It was a ballet based on music by his compatriot Stravinsky. Overnight, that work became an international musical sensation. For the rest of his life, which lasted until 1971, Stravinsky would remain one of the twentieth century's leading musicians. The list of great works stemming from his pen is extensive. It includes the *Rite of Spring*, *Pulcinella*, *Petrushka*, and *The Firebird*.

Craft wrote a great deal about his friend, his music, and various personal topics that came up during their countless conversations and dinner parties. For example, the composer once said, in connection with his place on the political spectrum: "I am opposed to the right, abhor the left, and am altogether out of sympathy with the center." His nuanced choice of words says a lot. But his other remarks and deeds—or lack thereof—are even more illuminating. At least, that's if we are to believe sources besides Craft: sources who unambiguously refer to the maestro as a man with fascist sympathies, a dislike of communism, and an aversion to Jewish people.

Stravinsky disliked communism. He had sympathized with the first wave of protest against the absolutist tsars, he even wrote a hymn of support, but the minute the revolution became a fact and the communists put the Soviet system in place, he became a fervent opponent. By then, he had long turned his back on his country: he only revisited Russia briefly in 1962. After leaving, Stravinsky lived and worked in several countries, beginning with Switzerland and France. In 1934, he became a French citizen.

Let us turn to the country that Stravinsky loved most: Italy. He had hoped to make it his first destination after leaving Russia. As luck would have it, things turned out differently. However, Stravinsky's love of Italy continued to smolder, and when Benito Mussolini came to power, it burned more brightly. King Victor Emanuel III of Italy offered Mussolini the position of prime minister following the riots during the fascist march on Rome in October 1922. Il Duce's first government was a coalition. But he quickly removed his opposition, and starting from 1924, he assumed total power. Everyone knows how that turned out: he became an absolute dictator.

However, in contrast with Hitler and his regime, Mussolini was tolerant of the modern arts, including music. Between 1925 and 1940, a great deal of attention was paid in Italy to the works of Béla Bartók, Darius Milhaud, Zoltán Kodály, Ernst Bloch, Paul Hindemith, Ernst Krenek, Arnold Schoenberg, Dmitri Shostakovich, as well as such performers as violinists Jacques Thibaud and Jascha Heifetz, cellist Pablo Casals, the African American singer Paul Robeson, and pianists Arthur Rubinstein, Arthur Schnabel, and Sergei Prokofiev. In other words, a group of artists who would have been shunned, expelled, persecuted, or murdered in the Third Reich for being Jewish, Slavic, anti-fascist, Bolshevik, modernistic, "degenerate," or foreign. To the Nazis, such terms were practically interchangeable. But in Italy, even during the war, many of the above performers still made the rounds. Because of their political stance, however, they were figures who you would not expect to see in the two largest Italian cultural metropolises — nor, for that matter, in any other Italian cities.

And yet, xenophobia and protectionism were already deeply ingrained in Italian culture. But apparently, that could go hand in hand with an appreciation of culture. Many saw this — incorrectly — as a sign that the Italian regime was exceptionally tolerant and progressive. Modern artists who were not very popular with the general public may have seen a chance to gain acceptance for their work and have it performed. It cannot, of course, be ruled out that Stravinsky was also duped by such a rosy prospect, but in his lip service, he went pretty far. In his book *Music in Fascist Italy*, the well-respected author Harvey Sachs describes Stravinsky's admiration for Il Duce. On the occasion of his first meeting with Mussolini, Stravinsky said the following to the well-known Italian music critic, Alberto Gasco: "I don't believe that anyone venerates Mussolini more than I do. To me he is the one man who counts nowadays in the whole world. I have traveled a great deal: I know many exalted personages, and my artist's mind does not shrink from political and social issues. Well, after having seen so many events and so many more or less representative men, I have an overpowering urge to render homage to your Duce. He is the savior of Italy and—let us hope—Europe."

That couldn't be clearer. After meeting Mussolini, Stravinsky reaffirmed what he'd previously said to Gasco and added that it had been one of the most beautiful moments of his life. Even Craft writes: "Stravinsky preferred Mussolini's fascism to British and French democracy." There is another such quote from Stravinsky after a meeting with Mussolini: "Unless my ears deceive me, the voice of Rome is the voice of Mussolini. I told him that I felt like a fascist myself." He later sent the dictator a copy of his *Duo Concertant*, his memoirs, and a gold medallion inscribed with an "expression of my deepest admiration for you and your work." One cannot be much more straightforward than that. So even if Stravinsky's actions were purely opportunistic, he could have toned it down and been more diplomatic.

Suspected of Being Jewish

During the Weimar Republic, Stravinsky often conducted his own compositions or worked as a pianist. The new music scene in Germany was thriving, especially during the final years of the Republic. Stravinsky continued to tour in Germany, both as a pianist and a conductor. He made recordings there throughout the 1930s. But, with the rise of the Nazi Party and the establishment in 1929 of the Kampfbund für Deutsche Kultur (Militant League for German Culture), resistance toward his performances grew. The grounds were both anti-modernist and anti-Semitic. The Nazis suspected that Stravinsky was Jewish. He came from Russia, was a foreigner, and possibly even a communist. What's more, he wrote those strange unfamiliar sounds. As a result, Stravinsky felt his popularity declining. In 1933, he wrote a letter to his publisher, Schott: "I am surprised to have received no proposals from Germany for next season." Even though his "negative attitude — not to put it in stronger terms — toward communism and Judaism was common knowledge."

Stravinsky demonstrated his admiration for fascism in other ways as well. He refused to sign a petition organized by conductor Otto Klemperer against the *Berufsverbote* affecting musicians in German orchestras. He turned a deaf ear to Arnold Schoenberg's pleas to help found a conservatory of music in Palestine. And he had no qualms about performing his Concerto for Two Pianos at the Baden-Baden International Festival of New Music, which had been organized by the Nazi Party. There, Stravinsky's work was displayed on a poster beside a piece by Paul Graener, the official Nazi composer, who from 1935 to 1941 was vice president of the Reich Music Chamber (Reichsmusikkammer). In 1938 in Düsseldorf, Stravinsky's entire body of works was included in the *Entartete Musik* (Degenerate Music) exhibition. He was up in arms and lodged a formal complaint with the German Ministry of Foreign Affairs: "My opponents go so far as to submit misleading insinuations that I am a Jew, ignorant of the fact that my ancestors were members of the Polish nobility."

Some years earlier, during the period of political transition, Stravinsky had made a similar claim. Using his family tree and other documents, he had proved he genuinely was not Jewish. Then to hammer home his point, he added: "I loathe all communism, Marxism, the execrable Soviet monster, and also all liberalism, democratism, atheism, etc."

There's another unexpected source: Stravinsky visited Belgium on numerous occasions. In December 1930, the celebrated composer stayed in Brussels for the world premiere of his *Symphony of Psalms*. The Boston Symphony Orchestra had commissioned him to write the piece to celebrate their fiftieth anniversary. As luck would have it, the Société Philharmonique de Bruxelles had the privilege of presenting the first performance, which took place in Brussels. The Swiss conductor and champion of new music Ernest Ansermet led the choir and orchestra. The concert was to take place on 13 December, and after the dress rehearsal in the Centre for Fine Arts the day before, Igor Stravinsky lunched with his famous compatriot Sergei Prokofiev. Prokofiev later noted in his diary: "Stravinsky never ceased to abuse the Jews. The chief object of his ire was Milhaud [Darius Milhaud, the celebrated French composer of Jewish descent]. Einstein is (to Stravinsky) a veritable synagogue yid."

Again, this entire Stravinsky episode illustrates how delicate historiography can be during wartime, especially in a cultural sense. Sometimes it's a question of sources that are conflicting or unclear. But generally, the sympathy or antipathy toward a person and their ideas influences the evaluation. The protagonists—like Stravinsky—have their sworn enemies and devoted friends, which can lead to a "yes-he-did-no-he-didn't" polemic. This is true in Stravinsky's case, as well.

Robert Craft, for example, tried to give a positive spin to Stravinsky's quotes, writings, and deeds. He presented counterarguments to quash or refute the opinions of dissenters. In his book Craft frequently sweeps Stravinsky's more incriminating quotes under the carpet. This casts a shadow over Craft's reliability. He uses the excuse that Stravinsky needed to secure his income and that working in Germany was important financially. According to Craft, Stravinsky had his back against the wall. This claim might stand up for ordinary German composers who depended on the income in their native country, and such fees could be interesting to foreign artists. But a celebrated international star like Igor Stravinsky would have been able to make a living anywhere, never mind a few dips in popularity. He left France in 1939 because his fashionableness had waned. He'd been lured to the United States by lucrative offers from institutions such as the Chicago Symphony Orchestra and Harvard University, and he later became a US citizen.

Craft also uses family elements to vindicate the musician. Stravinsky could not possibly be called anti-Semitic because he had a Jewish son-in-law named Yuri Mandelstam, who'd married his daughter Ludmila. This may be true, but according to Richard Taruskin, another American musicologist, Craft fails to mention that the Stravinskys had vehemently opposed the marriage. They displayed little enthusiasm at the birth of their first grandchild. Grandmother Stravinsky was more than a little relieved when she wrote to her husband, who was on tour, that the baby didn't look very Jewish. But she was nevertheless worried about how the infant's nose would develop. *Scripta manent* (the writings remain), but Craft refutes it.

When Stravinsky's daughter Ludmila became ill and was admitted to a sanatorium in the Haute-Savoie region of France, her husband didn't have enough money to stay with her. Apparently, Stravinsky never offered to help them. Not true, according to Craft, who claims that after Ludmila's death the composer paid his granddaughter a considerable annual sum of four hundred thousand dollars. It's thought that Stravinsky also held Yuri Mandelstam's poetry in high regard. But, of course, Craft was not impartial: he owed a great deal of his career's success and fame to his friendship with the composer.

Speaking of poems: in 1951–1952, Stravinsky composed his Cantata for solo voices, choir, and instrumental ensemble. Much has been said about the English poems from the fifteenth and sixteenth centuries on which the work is based. W. H. Auden gave Stravinsky the idea of using the poems he had published. Many consider the material to be an expression of anti-Semitism. In the second ricercar, Taruskin sees the verse "To-morrow Shall Be My Dancing Day" as an assertion that the Jews were responsible for Christ's death. In his opinion that's going pretty far, just seven years after the Holocaust. But reading the poems with the knowledge that W. H. Auden had selected them, and knowing that he collaborated on the work, makes such claims difficult if not impossible to swallow. Here, Craft does seem to have the right idea: it's splitting hairs to search for an anti-Semitic statement in that composition. However, that's not to say that Stravinsky had suddenly become enamored of Jewish people.

Although Craft tries to suggest as much by pointing out that Stravinsky, in 1962, conducted in Israel, and that in 1964, he wrote another cantata, *Abraham and Isaac*, based on a Hebrew text. But this can hardly be used as an argument: Stravinsky was not a simpleton! This all took place in the middle of the postwar period. All the horrors had been revealed. It had long been a mortal sin — and inopportune, especially in a commercial sense — to portray the composer as anti-Semitic or a friend of the fascist movement. As a recently naturalized American, Stravinsky understood he had to change his tune. The man who once hated democracy even embraced the Democratic Party.

Stravinsky's friendship with the violinist Samuel Dushkin, born in Poland of Jewish origin, has also been trotted out in his defense, along with Stravinsky's refusal to conduct a concert in Turin, Italy, because the radio network had refused to broadcast a piano concerto written by a Jewish composer, Vittorio Rieti. But those are exceptions that do not outweigh the charges against the defendant. As an argument in his defense, Stravinsky's friendship with another Russian émigré, Arthur Lourié, is considerably less persuasive. In Paris, Lourié, who was Jewish, became a helpful assistant and major champion of Stravinsky's work, and Stravinsky benefited from their contact. Between 1924 and 1931, Lourié was a member of Stravinsky's inner circle, although the two later parted company. Earlier in Paris, Stravinsky had contributed to the bimonthly avant-garde magazine *Montjoie!*, which had racist, anti-Semitic, and undemocratic leanings.

It is clear that Stravinsky wanted to have little to do with Jewish people, and his published letters are full of sneers aimed at them. He even referred to the Russian Revolution as a Jewish plague. Some members of the pro-Stravinsky camp offer a simple explanation: "Isn't anti-Semitism part of every Russian's nature? So why shouldn't it be part of Stravinsky's?" Such reasoning certainly didn't apply to his teacher, Nikolai Rimsky-Korsakov, who enthusiastically supported the marriage of his daughter to a Jewish musician. And with this, we seamlessly approach what is perhaps the crux of the problem: a musician named Maximilian Steinberg.

According to both Mr. Craft and Mr. Taruskin, therein

lies the genuine source (or one of many sources?) of Stravinsky's anti-Semitic sentiment. A youthful trauma, as it were. They both attended the Saint Petersburg Conservatory, studying first with Rimsky-Korsakov and later with Alexander Glazunov. At the time, Steinberg was the absolute darling of the entire conservatory, while Stravinsky hardly got a second look. The vain and revengeful Stravinsky would never have been able to cope with that. Life can be so simple.

Bronisław Huberman
Public Enemy Number One

Bronisław Huberman, known affectionately as the "Oskar Schindler of music," was a violinist born to a Jewish family in Poland. His name appears on more or less every list of "the best violinists of all time," along with such masters as Leonid Kogan, Fritz Kreisler, Isaac Stern, Gidon Kremer, and the Belgians Arthur Grumiaux and Eugène Ysaye, to name just a few. Hitler also had a high regard for Huberman. In his Berlin bunker, Hitler cherished his recordings made by the man who, like Schindler, saved countless Jewish lives. But, of course, the comparison is limited to Schindler's humanitarian qualities. It seems that Schindler, an industrialist, may have played a much less attractive role when, as a spy for the German Abwehr intelligence service and a member of the Nazi Party, he helped implement Operation Gleiwitz, thereby paving the way for Hitler's 1939 invasion of Poland.

Bronisław Huberman had an almost enchanted childhood. He was born into a wealthy family in Często-chowa, Poland, in 1882. As a wunderkind he first began

studying in Warsaw and Paris. At the age of eleven, he moved to Berlin to take lessons from the legendary violinist Joseph Joachim, another illustrious name from the list of great violinists. Huberman's career took off. One year later, Huberman began touring Europe, both with chamber music ensembles and as a soloist with orchestras. He gave his first major foreign concert with the Berlin Philharmonic Orchestra on tour in the Netherlands, in the Kurzaal in the Dutch city of Scheveningen. Appearances in other cities soon followed, including Brussels, where Huberman left an unforgettable impression by playing a virtuosic violin concerto by the Belgian composer Henri Vieuxtemps (another name from the list of greats). Brussels is also where he met the piano wonder Arthur Rubinstein, who was then six years old. The two became lifelong friends. As a promising young violinist, Huberman continued to tour through the rest of Europe and North America. Two years later, when he was just fourteen, he felt that his education was complete.

He decided to start conquering the music world as an adult, along with his violin, of course. That instrument was the Gibson Stradivarius, built in 1713, and named for its former owner. The Polish Count Zamoyski gave Huberman the violin as a gift, which was presented by the Austrian emperor Franz Joseph during a performance in Paris. With such a violin, Huberman was well equipped to embark upon his professional career. Carnegie Hall,

La Scala, the Musikverein in Vienna: he conquered them all in record time. One highlight from that early period was undoubtedly a performance in Vienna in 1896, where Huberman played the Brahms Violin Concerto in the presence of Gustav Mahler, Johann Strauss, Antonin Dvořák, and no one less than the composer himself.

In 1920, deeply affected by the atrocities of the First World War, Huberman interrupted his nomadic existence. He had become so profoundly obsessed with politics that he took time away from the concert stage to study social and political sciences at the Sorbonne. Once there, he immediately joined the Paneuropean Union, a movement devoted to European countries' political, social, and military unification. The organization was the initiative of Count Richard von Coudenhove-Kalergi, a descendant of the Flemish "van" Coudenhove family that had fled to Austria during the French Revolution. The Paneuropean Union was a forerunner of the European Union. Its members, appalled by the horrors of the First World War, aimed to develop a peaceful economic union in Europe, one that could stand up to other major world powers. Von Coudenhove was later nominated for the Nobel Peace Prize. He was responsible, in 1955, for suggesting Ludwig van Beethoven's "Ode to Joy" as a European anthem. Thomas Mann, Albert Einstein, and Konrad Adenauer were also involved in the Paneuropean movement. It seems likely that Huberman, born into a

Jewish family, felt at home with such gentlemen, who promoted mixing races and classes.

After completing his studies at the Sorbonne, Huberman picked up where he'd left off in his thriving solo career. But everywhere he played, he shared his ideas about the Paneuropean Union. In 1934 he was appointed the director of the University of Music and Performing Arts in Vienna, but he continued to concertize. He refused every invitation to play in Germany, however, despite conductor Wilhelm Furtwängler's pleas for him to appear at the opening concert of the 1934–1935 season.

The Promised Land

Huberman's violin has its own tale to tell and is a crucial chapter in his life story. It seems that his treasured Stradivarius had a turbulent history. The instrument was stolen and recovered twice. The most recent occurrence was in 1936, when Huberman was immersed in the project that earned him his "Schindler" nickname. Huberman had played in Palestine on concert tours in 1929 and 1931. There, he discovered that cultural life was practically nonexistent, so he decided to help set up a Palestine Symphony Orchestra. His plan was to convince Jewish musicians who had positions in German orchestras and other major European cities to move to Palestine. Unfortunately, his scheme didn't get off the ground.

First, the region held little cultural or economic appeal for such high-caliber artists. And second, few suspected that within a few years, the *Berufsverbot* would result in musicians being brutally kicked out of their orchestras or, worse, ending up in concentration camps. To get the entire project up and running, Huberman had to contend with another massive problem: He needed a lot of money. It would be no mean feat to house the musicians and their families and pay their wages. Travel and relocation expenses were high, and the concert infrastructure had to be developed.

The artistic challenges diminished after 1933 when German musicians started losing their orchestra jobs. Suddenly, they could see the threat hanging over their heads. Nevertheless, many wanted to remain in Germany. Some joined what was then called the Kulturbund Deutscher Juden (Cultural Federation of German Jews, or Kubu, later known as the Jüdischer Kulturbund). That organization was intended for unemployed Jewish performing artists who had been sidelined by the government. These musicians were still permitted to get together and perform, as long as it wasn't in a German institution. But of course, there wasn't much left over: Jewish musicians could only perform for Jewish audiences. But they hoped the situation would improve.

That hope, however, was short-lived. During the Reichstag of 1935, the Nürnberger Gesetze (Nuremberg

Laws) were passed, stripping Jewish citizens of their rights. The laws later extended to include the Black population and the Romani people. Huberman responded with a heartfelt open letter published in the *Manchester Guardian*, aimed at German intellectuals who had failed to react to what was happening. Here is one sentence from that letter: "Before the whole world I accuse you, German intellectuals, you non-Nazis, as those truly guilty for all these Nazi crimes, all this lamentable breakdown of a great people."

Huberman renewed his efforts to make his dream of an orchestra in Palestine a reality. He convinced David Ben-Gurion, the leader of the Jewish community and, later, the first prime minister, to shelter seventy musicians and their families. Huberman recruited these musicians from orchestras throughout Europe. The advancing storm was ever more visible, even beyond the German border. He asked wealthy Jewish patrons in Great Britain and the United States to donate the necessary funds. In 1936 Huberman made a marathon benefit tour of the United States.

While he was onstage in Carnegie Hall playing his other priceless violin, a Guarneri "del Gesu," someone stole his Stradivarius from the dressing room. Huberman never saw his treasured instrument again. It remained untraceable until 1985 when, on his deathbed, Julian Altman confessed to his wife, Marcelle Hall, that he had stolen the violin. Altman had been a vaudeville violinist appearing in clubs and cafés in New York. At the time of the robbery he played with a gypsy-style orchestra in the Russian Bear, a club just behind Carnegie Hall. When the widow decided to return the violin to Lloyd's of London, its rightful owner, she demanded a finder's fee of $250,000. A prolonged legal tussle followed. Finally, in 2001, the celebrated American violinist Joshua Bell, also of Jewish descent, paid the paltry sum of $4,000,000 for the instrument. He now performs spectacular concerts on that violin.

Huberman wasn't deterred by the robbery. He continued on his tour and managed to raise the necessary funds. In addition to donations and the proceeds from concerts, money was also raised with expensive dinners, one of which was organized in New York by Albert Einstein. The two gentlemen sometimes played music together, which leads to an amusing anecdote: Einstein was an amateur violinist, and once, they were playing Bach's Double Concerto. That was at another benefit concert for scientists persecuted by the Nazis. Unfortunately, Einstein missed his entrance, and apparently, Huberman turned to the great scholar and Nobel laureate and said: "Know what your problem is? You can't count to three!" They managed, in any event to raise enough money to get the project off the ground.

The visas for the European orchestral musicians were

secured through the World Zionist Organization, and an orchestra was born. The Palestine Symphony Orchestra was made up of Jewish musicians from Germany and other European locations ranging from Budapest to Amsterdam. It later became the Israel Philharmonic Orchestra. The orchestra's first concert took place on 26 December 1936. Filmmaker Josh Aronson recently made a gripping documentary called *Orchestra of Exiles* about the events leading up to the orchestra's beginnings. Huberman, for his part, could not have found a more fitting conductor for the first season than Arturo Toscanini. The program consisted of music by Carl Maria von Weber, Gioachino Rossini, Johannes Brahms, Franz Schubert, and — inevitably — the Jewish composer Felix Mendelssohn, whose music had been banned in Germany.

Huberman's initiative killed two birds with one stone. He had improved the cultural life in Israel while saving the lives of thousands of Jewish musicians and their families. Or was it three birds? That's certainly true if one reads Huberman's quote: "One has to build a fist against anti-Semitism. A first-class orchestra will be this fist!" The Nazi regime must have felt the blow, because among all the world's musicians the party labeled Huberman "the greatest enemy of the Nazis." He would have been honored.

Anton Webern
A Forgotten Cult Figure

Anton Webern remains for a select and somewhat limited audience one of the most significant musical cult figures of the classical twentieth century. He was born in 1883 in the Löwengasse in Vienna. His father, Carl, was a civil-servant mining engineer. His mother, Amelie, was a housewife and a reasonably proficient amateur pianist and singer. The family had been members of the aristocracy since 1574. After the 1918 revolution in Austria, the distinction "von" was outlawed. But Anton Webern pursued a career in music, where no distinctive "von" was needed. The family spent some years in Graz and Klagenfurt because of father Webern's career. It was in Klagenfurt that Anton received his earliest musical training, and he played the cello in a local orchestra.

After returning to Vienna in 1902, he studied musicology with Guido Adler at Vienna University. Two years after graduating, he became one of Arnold Schoenberg's private students. Like Alban Berg, his contemporary, he became acquainted with and adhered to his teacher's

atonal or twelve-tone technique. That system, at times overly complex for audiences to comprehend, can be compared with abstract painting. It is a seemingly random sequence of notes in which the average listener hears little or no connection, let alone melody. Webern's compositions were not especially popular, and so to make ends meet he embarked upon a conducting career.

Wrong Time, Wrong Place?

Sadly, we will never know if Webern would have become a great maestro. Starting from 1908, he conducted several modest theater orchestras—in Bad Ischl, Gdansk, Teplice, Stettin, and Prague. He was obliged to conduct operettas—which he considered beneath him—and he was soon bored with the tedious routine of the theater, so he quit. He felt the only true art was in the creative work of composition. Some years later, he would again pick up his conductor's baton. In that second period, he led such organizations as the Mödlinger Choral Society and the workers' symphony concerts of the Social Democratic Art Space in Vienna—a left-leaning organization. He also regularly conducted one of the radio orchestras. Gradually, in the 1920s and 1930s, Webern became more well known.

In 1934 a controversy forced him to resign from his Mödling choral conducting position: he'd hired a Jewish singer to replace one of the ailing choir members. It seems that, at the time, an anti-Semitic frenzy was raging through the Austrian capital, and fascism was on the rise. Webern suffered the consequences, even though he was not politically active. In 1933 the Austrian Nazi leaders had mistakenly labeled him "a Jew" because of his "reprehensible" atonality: such artistic monstrosities could only arise from a sick, degenerate, Jewish mind. After the Anschluss, the situation worsened. During the famous "degenerate music" exhibition in Düsseldorf in May 1938 the organizer, Hans Ziegler, called the music of the modernists "a product of the Jewish spirit." Webern and others were rather conveniently but inaccurately grouped together with Jewish composers. And so, the leaders of the new regime quickly had Webern in their sights. Richard Strauss, the former chairman of the Reich Chamber of Music, was strongly opposed to political attempts to interfere with the aesthetic norms of musical expression. He thought it was up to listeners to pass judgment on a composition's merits (yet more evidence that Strauss was not a fervent Nazi). Be that as it may, Webern watched the publication and performances of his works dwindle. He no longer had any private students, his conducting career was over, and he had to accept odd jobs to pay the bills. In 1940 Webern earned no monthly income at all. So he wrote piano arrangements for other, less-well-known composers. He also worked as an editor and proofreader for his publisher, Universal Edition.

Schoenberg fled to the United States immediately after Hitler assumed power in Austria, but Webern stayed behind in Vienna, where he risked sinking into obscurity. In fact, he may not have made it into the footnotes of music history had it not been for the intervention of some authoritative postwar musicians, most notably the French composer and conductor Pierre Boulez and the German avant-gardist Karl-Heinz Stockhausen. They took an interest in Webern and his music. Thanks to their efforts on his behalf, Webern later assumed his rightful third place in the holy trinity of what's known as the Second Viennese School, alongside Berg and Schoenberg. (At the risk of being pedantic: the First Viennese School is the name given to the classical-romantic era of Mozart, Haydn, and Beethoven.)

It is fair to say that Webern's often cerebral works still remain impenetrable to vast members of the general public. He tried to say as much as possible with a limited number of notes, and he paid great attention to silence. However, the only titles that still crop up from time to time in concerts are *Im Sommerwind* and *Passacaglia*, orchestral works written in the more conventional, late romantic style, along with a few of his art songs. Other titles that come to mind include the "Fuga (Ricercata) a 6 voci," based on Bach's *Musical Offering* and (believe it or not) a brilliant arrangement for chamber ensemble of the "Schatz-Walzer" by the ebullient waltz king Johann Strauss. Not the first thing you might expect from him.

Sadly, Webern was unable to experience the resurgence of his popularity among a select group of professional musicians and new music enthusiasts. He died on 15 September 1945. It's conceivable that the circumstances surrounding his death contributed to renewed interest. The tale is both moving and gripping, but there are several versions.

At first sight, Webern could be mistaken for another victim of that depraved regime. And yet, he would without doubt have preferred to be appreciated while he was still alive. Against his better judgment, he thought and hoped that the new regime emerging in Germany would also provide his country with stability, security, work, and more attention for him personally. Could it be that some of his remarks in favor of the system were based on his convictions? In any case, there were times when he clearly expressed himself in terms of support. One source even calls him the most unashamed Hitler enthusiast among the league of German Austrian composers. When Germany invaded Denmark and Norway in 1940, his reaction was unambiguous: "This is the Germany of today! The National Socialist Germany, of course. This is the new state whose seed was planted twenty years ago. Yes indeed, a state like never before! It is nothing new! But a creation of this unique man!!! It becomes more exciting every day. I see a beautiful future. For me as well, everything will be different."

Webern's son Peter took action and joined the Nazi Party. Webern himself suffered from a Germanic sense of superiority, and his attitude toward foreign composers influenced his lectures. According to the American composer Roland Leich, who studied with Webern in Vienna in 1933–1934, Webern described foreign composers as watered-down versions of greater German examples. Hector Berlioz was just a French Ludwig van Beethoven, Peter Tchaikovsky was a Russian Robert Schumann, and Sir Edward Elgar was an English Felix Mendelssohn. He went further still when he said: "It's only the superior old German culture that can save this world from the demoralized condition into which it has been thrown." That is a quote from a conversation the composer had with Ukrainian-born violinist Louis Krasner, who commissioned many works from composers of the Second Viennese School. When Krasner asked if someone like Hitler was the answer, Webern replied: "Who knows if these excesses we've been reading about are real? As far as I'm concerned, that's propaganda!" An example of the classic *Wir haben es nicht gewusst*: We didn't know what was happening.

And yet, except for the lip service mentioned above,

Webern never really supported the regime. A familiar story. One can't really accuse Webern of anti-Semitism, either. He often worked with Jewish musicians and didn't discriminate. See his hiring of a Jewish choral singer in Mödling, and his close bond with his best friend and guru, Arnold Schoenberg, a Zionist. Yet nevertheless, Louis Krasner remembers Webern saying, "Even Schoenberg would have been entirely different if he had not been Jewish."

Webern's Death: Three Versions

Returning to the events of 15 September 1945. The "romantic" version is believed by hard-core Webern fans: The war was over, and the composer was enjoying sitting at the door of his house in Mittersill, near Salzburg. He was relaxed and content after the preceding horrible years. During the final weeks of the war, he had moved to the Salzburg region, where two of his three daughters had settled, fleeing the approaching Russians. He was quietly smoking a cigar. Its tip lit up every time he inhaled, and an American soldier from North Carolina named Raymond Norwood Bell ordered him — in English — to put it out. There was a ban at the time on both light and fire. Webern, who spoke no English, did not understand the command. When the soldier asked Webern to put out his cigar for the third time, Webern still did nothing. So the soldier shot him. One might be inclined to think this was an unfortunate coincidence resulting in the absurd death of a great, innocent artist. Following the incident, Webern's colleagues and admirers, including the progressive "cultural Bolshevik" Ernst Krenek, who himself had been a target of the Nazis, elevated Webern to quasi-hero status. But is this the truth or not? In Webern's case, the answer is more complicated than on a glitzy quiz show.

According to reports, the story of what really happened is somewhat less innocent. Webern went to Mittersill to get away from the horrors of war and mourn his son's recent death on the Russian front. Fed up with the war and devastated by the painful loss of their son, Webern and his wife, Wilhelmine, left Vienna and traveled—sometimes on foot—to their two daughters Christine and Maria. Their third daughter, Amalie, was there as well. In Mittersill, Webern's spirits began to improve. He received news that he would be allowed to keep his job teaching composition at the Vienna Academy and would be able to conduct the radio orchestra again. In September 1945, the Americans occupied Salzburg, and they soon clamped down on the black market. But Webern's son-in-law—Christine's husband, Benno Mattel—had gotten involved with shady dealings. One evening, a few American soldiers, posing as potential customers for his black market provisions, were chatting with Benno in the kitchen. Benno fell into their trap and was arrested. Raymond Norwood Bell, the American company's cook, later said that Webern attacked him after Benno's arrest. That's not entirely inconceivable: Webern had finally found some peace and quiet, the family had been reunited, the clouds were lifting, and suddenly there was a setback. And so Webern came to the defense of his family member. What's more, it is possible that Webern, with his pan-Germanic views, saw the American liberators as invaders. There are many hypotheses to explain the disparate versions of the incident. But in all of them, it was Bell who pulled the trigger.

A third version, somewhere between the two above, probably comes closest to the truth. The musicologist Hans Moldenhauer delved into the records fifteen years after the occurrence and ran up against the same conflicting versions. He concluded that Webern and his wife had gone to dinner at their daughter Christine's that evening. After the meal, Webern withdrew—with a cigar, as mentioned in all the versions—while the Americans negotiated with Benno. Bell hadn't realized that other people were in the house, so when he heard footsteps, he went to investigate. After that, Webern stumbled in, bleeding. *"Es ist aus!"* "It's over" were his last words. Moldenhauer does not believe that Webern would physically have assaulted Bell. Why would a frail, unarmed man, barely five foot tall and weighing 110 pounds, attack a healthy American soldier? Molden-hauer's research became the basis of an opera, *The Death of Webern*, by composer Michael Dellaira and librettist J. D. McClatchy.

But the outcome remained the same: Webern met his death in a rather senseless way. As did Bell, who was plagued for the rest of his life by Webern's death, especially once he realized precisely whom he had killed. Bell tried to drown his sorrows and died in 1955 of alcoholism. According to Bell's wife, whenever Bell got drunk, he felt remorse for the events of the evening of 15 September.

Olivier Messiaen
The Composer Ornithologist

Theresienstadt was not the only camp where music was played. It happened in many other concentration and labor camps, generally under horrific circumstances. However, under those conditions, outstanding works were rarely produced. Prisoners had to make do with the means at their disposal: a limited selection of instruments, often in poor condition; a few trained musicians, but mostly amateurs; and little if any sheet music or scores. One of the exceptions was a quartet for a rather unusual combination of instruments by Olivier Messiaen, one of the most significant musicians of the twentieth century.

He was a Frenchman, born in Avignon in 1908, but his surname indicates that he was of Flemish origin, specifically from the Wervik region. His grandfather was married to Flavie Demyttenaere, another clearly Flemish name. There are still many Messiaens in east and west Flanders. Olivier's father, Pierre, was married to the French poet Cécile Sauvage and taught English

at various educational institutions in Nantes, Paris, and Avignon. He was also responsible for a French translation of Shakespeare. Olivier grew up in a cultured Catholic household, and his decision to play the organ was no surprise. When he was in his early twenties, he was named the organist—in command of a Cavaillé-Coll organ—in one of the most important churches in Paris, the Église de la Sainte-Trinité. He soon gained a reputation for his incredible improvisations, and he held on to his position in the church until he died in 1992. The war broke out when Messiaen was in his early thirties. As a composer, he had already attracted attention with a few of his works. His *Poèmes pour Mi* (Mi was his nickname for his then wife, Claire Delbos) is still his most frequently performed work from that era.

A Passion for Birds

From the beginning, Messiaen was attracted to progressive ideas in music. He did not want to continue the traditions that had preceded him and preferred to seek inspiration in Hindu rhythms. He was equally unwilling to jump on the bandwagon of that era's musical fads, including a flirtation with jazz. In fact, his most important source of inspiration was as old as the hills: religious sentiment, which fit like a glove with his love of Gregorian chant.

Another thread that runs through his entire body of work is his fascination with bird sounds. In French he even referred to himself as a *compositeur ornithologiste*, or composer ornithologist. When describing composers, it's no wonder he is known as the "one with the birds." He trekked into the great outdoors to tape-record bird-song or jot down avian melodies on a musical staff. He would then use those sounds in his compositions, either quoting them literally or as a starting point for personal creation. Two of the most impressive pieces of his are the monumental symphony *Turangalîla* and a chamber work for four instruments, which is the subject of this chapter. This is another story with several versions, and depending on the source, the accent is placed on slightly different aspects.

In 1939 Messiaen was mobilized and assigned to a medical unit with a military music division in Verdun. However, in 1940, somewhere near Nancy in northwestern France, he was taken prisoner. In his book *Images*, Messiaen's father, Pierre, described the events. Olivier had been on his bicycle, riding to Epinal with two small boxes of manuscripts and sheet music strapped to the luggage rack when German soldiers captured him. He first spent ten days in a filthy garage in Nancy. It was hot and it smelled. There was no latrine, and all the food was canned. Messiaen then spent ten additional days in a transit camp: conditions there weren't much better. This version is still from the colorful introduction written by Messiaen's father. Among the other prisoners were two French musicians, one of whom, the cellist Etienne Pasquier, had been Messiaen's superior in the army camp in Verdun. For many years after the war he performed in a celebrated trio with his brothers Jean (violin) and Pierre (viola), until his death in 1997. The other musician was a clarinetist named Henri Akoka. In the last French camp in Toul, near Nancy, Messiaen wrote a solo work for Akoka, called "Abîme des oiseaux." Some maintain that Henri Akoka played the piece outdoors while they were awaiting transport. They were then sent in cattle cars to Görlitz in the Prussian province of Silesia. Based again on his father's account, we learn that Messiaen, on arrival, developed dysentery, forcing him to spend a month in the hospital. It was a primitive facility where Polish nuns looked after him. Images of Hitler were hanging on the walls, oddly conspicuous among the crucifixes and pictures of the Virgin Mary.

The Stalag

Eventually, all three arrived at Stalag 8-A in Görlitz. There, they met another compatriot, the violinist Jean Le Boulaire. Görlitz is a "twin" city: the Polish half, Zgorzelec, is on the eastern bank of the Neisse River, while the German half, Görlitz, is on the western bank.

The German word *Stalag* is a contraction of *STAmmLAGer für kriegsgefangene Mannschaften und Unteroffiziere* (prison camp for noncommissioned prisoners of war). The camp in Görlitz was initially intended for Hitler Youth and was near the Wehrmacht's exercise grounds. In 1939 the center was converted to a prison for Poles. It had about forty pitch-roofed barracks lined up in a row. A double roll of barbed wire surrounded the entire terrain; there were two electrified entry gates and ten watchtowers manned by guards. Although the camp was designed to contain a maximum of 25,000 prisoners, at times it housed as many as 50,000 inmates who were primarily put to work in machine factories, the glass industry, and in helping farmers in the surrounding countryside. Later in the war the camp became a genuine slaughterhouse where no fewer than 16,000 Russians lost their lives through hardship, disease, or murder. When Messiaen and his three companions ended up there, most of the other prisoners were Frenchmen and Belgians captured on the Western Front. According to statistics, there were 23,582 prisoners there at that time.

The prisoners were not all treated alike. Those from a western *Kulturnation* (cultural nation) such as Belgium or France were allowed some privileges. After work they could read a newspaper or visit a sports field or an assembly hall for lectures, theater, music, and even jazz nights. But prisoners from eastern Europe faced nothing but misery and, ultimately, death. Messiaen was doubly blessed, because he came from a culturally developed country, and the camp was ruled by officers, some of whom were greater fans of music than of Hitler. One music-loving guard was named Carl-Albert Brüll. He made sure the "French Mozart" did not have to get his hands dirty. On the contrary, he provided Messiaen with pencils, an eraser, and enough paper to compose music. That was more than what many free German composers had at their disposal. A piano was also made available. Messiaen, alone in a guarded room, had a regular supply of sandwiches and enough peace and quiet to work on a trio for his fellow prisoners. The jailors casually advised Messiaen and his colleagues not to try to escape, ostensibly because they'd be better off in Görlitz than in France under the Vichy regime. When Akoka nevertheless toyed with the idea of making a run for it he suggested that Messiaen join him. The composer replied that it was God's will he should be locked up.

Messiaen had carefully saved the small piece "Abîme des oiseaux," and it became the point of departure for his new piece. The movement entitled "Louange à l'éternité de Jésus" was based on an existing work. He added six additional movements. A piano was available, so he decided to take advantage of the circumstances and compose a piano part. The result: the eight-movement *Quatuor pour la fin du temps* (*Quartet for the End of Time*).

The camp leaders gave the four musicians ample oppor-tunity to rehearse: after 6:00 p.m., when their work was done, and in the washroom. The world premiere took place on 15 January 1941, not in a festive concert hall with music critics, VIPs, or snobs. Instead, the concert was held in a partly covered barracks. Some of the motley audience members, made up of four hundred guards and prisoners, were forced to stand outside in the rain. None was dressed in their Sunday best, and tickets cost twenty Reichspfennig. Messiaen would later say that he had "never been listened to with such rapt attention and comprehension" as in that camp.

This observation crops up repeatedly in descriptions of musical performances in the camps. No surprise, con-sidering that music often provided the only moment of peace, comfort, beauty, and hope in inmates' lives. How-ever, even for those in the know, Messiaen's composition is hardly an easy ride. Listeners might wrongly suspect that the Nazis would have clamped down on the work as being degenerate or *entartet*. Yet nothing could have been further from the truth. The performance of the *Quartet for the End of Time* went ahead without a hitch.

Quartet for the End of Time

It seems probable that the ears of some of those chance lis-teners were buzzing from the sometimes confusing and chaotic sounds. Perhaps the sonorities even reminded them of the horrors of war, and if so they may have associated the serene, quiet closing movement with the ending of hostilities and peace. In the piece, Messiaen consciously used birdsong as an inspiration for the first time — namely, a blackbird and a nightingale, played by the clarinet in "Abîme des oiseaux." Open-minded and curious listeners may have heard and understood the symbolism: one bird is free, and the other is caged. However, in Messiaen's spoken introduction preceding the premiere, he said the work referred exclusively to the biblical end of time. Of course, he would also have realized that, under the circumstances, it would have been inopportune to give the impression he saw a parallel between the peace of the Last Judgment and the reality of war. In any event, Messiaen's preface to the score has remained unchanged: "And the angel which I saw stand upon the sea and upon the earth lifted up his hand to heaven, and swore by him that liveth for ever and ever that there should be time no longer: But in the days of the voice of the seventh angel, when he shall begin to sound, the mystery of God should be finished."

Every story has its own history and discrepancies. In the 1990s I was lucky enough to interview an eyewitness, Etienne Pasquier, in his apartment in Paris for the Belgian VRT television network. I was in the company of the outstanding cellist Roel Dieltiens. At the time

Pasquier was almost ninety, but he was still lucid and enthusiastic. Despite all his sympathy and admiration for Messiaen as a musician, he felt compelled to say he had the distinct impression that his companion had, in a manner of speaking, romanticized, cultivated, or even *commercialized* the entire Stalag episode, although he stopped short of saying that explicitly. Messiaen, according to Pasquier, liked to call attention to the miserable circumstances: the cold, the rain, the threadbare clothing, and the horrible condition of the instruments. It was indeed cold. But take that ostensibly broken-down piano: in Pasquier's opinion, it didn't sound so bad. Messiaen also claimed that Pasquier's cello only had three strings, when in fact the cellist had been allowed to leave the camp to buy a brand-new instrument in town. According to Pasquier, their fate could have been much worse, especially when compared with what others endured. They were well looked after, were exempt from heavy labor, and were allowed to make music to their hearts' content. Some accounts report that more than five thousand people attended that first concert. Messiaen spoke of an audience of ten thousand, but Pasquier estimated the number to be closer to four hundred. Some of Messiaen's contemporaries and countrymen found him somewhat uncritical about his own work. But anyone who has ever spent even half a day in such a camp must deserve forgiveness.

Messiaen was released in February 1941. The circumstances are not entirely clear. Rumor has it that the camp guard Brüll slipped Messiaen the necessary forged and stamped papers. While still interned, Messiaen had sent word to the world-famous pianist Alfred Cortot, whom the pro-German Vichy government had just appointed high commissioner for the arts. Messiaen likely got in touch with Cortot to find work after his release. His friends deny it; his critics do not. In March–April of that same year, Messiaen was appointed professor of harmony at the Paris Conservatory. Oh, discord! The position Messiaen filled had been left vacant by André Bloch who, along with the entire faculty of Jewish teachers, had been fired.

A few months after its premiere, the *Quartet for the End of Time* was performed in Paris by the same musicians, except for Henri Akoka, who was still in the camp. While Brull's forged papers had secured the release of the other three colleagues, they didn't work for Akoka. Another guard spotted Akoka's Semitic features and decided to keep him imprisoned. Shortly after that, Akoka nevertheless escaped by jumping onto a moving train. He died of cancer in 1976. Jean Le Boulaire left his career in music and in 1943 became an actor. He had parts in dozens of films, including *Cartouche* with Jean-Paul Belmondo and several French detective series. He died in Paris in 1999.

For the rest of the occupation years, Messiaen remained

somewhat aloof. But of course, he had a wife and child to support, and therefore he needed security. This explains why his circle of friends included figures like René Dommange — the head of his publishing house, Durand — who had actively collaborated with the enemy as a politician. Messiaen also needed permission from the German government to perform his concerts. But one thing is certain: he never took up an explicitly pro-German position, and he had a lot of contact with those from the extreme left and the Resistance. In fact, Messiaen never besmirched his reputation as a Frenchman. In the cemetery of Saint-Théoffrey, near Grenoble, he waits patiently for the End of Time.

Anita Lasker
A Little-Known but Noble Woman

Every music lover is familiar with Anton Webern, but few have heard of Anita Lasker. She is by no means a household name in the music world, but her achievements during and after the war are awe-inspiring. She became a highly regarded solo cellist and a successful composer of film scores and soundtracks. Her father, Alfons, was a modestly successful lawyer in Breslau, Germany, in what is now Wrocław. He was a man with an excellent singing voice. Her mother, Edith, was a housewife and a serviceable violinist. Their three daughters grew up surrounded by music: Anita, born in 1925, and her sisters, Marianne and Renate. The Laskers were a close-knit, well respected, prosperous, and—in their own eyes—well-assimilated, unorthodox Jewish family. They were blissfully unaware of any external threats, although there were plenty. During the First World War, Alfons fought bravely in the German army and was awarded an Iron Cross. Music was a crucial part of daily

life in their home: the three sisters formed a classical piano trio, and the parents liked to join in.

Turbulent Times on the Horizon

Starting from 1933 the Laskers had to contend with growing harassment from the Nazis. When she was eight, Anita remembered how a classmate grabbed the eraser out of her hand when she was about to wipe the blackboard: "Jews are not allowed to have the eraser!" She never forgot that spiteful sentence, nor being called a "filthy Jew," or the signs proclaiming, *Juden unerwünscht* (Jews are unwanted here), or being spit upon in the street. The violence escalated, and Jewish women were required to add "Sarah" to their signatures; it was "Israel" for the men. Professional bans increased, and forced relocations grew in number. Everything led up to the climax in November 1938: Kristallnacht.

Still, it took the Lasker family a while to accept that turbulent times were on the horizon. Their father remained convinced it would all blow over and that the Germans would get the lunacy out of their system. He couldn't have been more wrong: things only got worse. In the end the Laskers made every effort to send their daughters to a safe country and to emigrate themselves. But by then, the Kafkaesque applications for and refusals of travel passes and delays in other documents made fleeing impossible.

While all this was going on, Anita tried to develop her talent as a cellist, but in Wrocław she couldn't find anyone willing to teach a Jewish girl. So in 1938 she moved to Berlin to take private lessons with a professor. There, the war soon took her — and everyone else — by surprise. Marianne was the only sister who managed to reach England before 3 September 1939, when France and Great Britain declared war on Nazi Germany. The rest of the family remained behind in Wrocław, still quietly hopeful — perhaps even optimistically expecting — that soon it would all blow over. Instead, Anita's cello was shoved to one side. In 1942 Anita and her sister were assigned work in a paper factory. They spent long days far from home, sticking labels onto toilet paper rolls. Anita wrote a surprisingly cheerful letter to her sister Marianne, saying she had more talent for sticking labels than playing the cello. Her Jewish sense of humor hadn't flagged. Renate worked in the napkin department. In that same year, their parents were arrested. It's thought they died in a massacre near Lublin, among a group of prisoners who were forced to dig their own graves before being shot.

Anita didn't stop at gluing labels. She and her sister also surreptitiously forged documents that allowed their French fellow prisoners to return to France. In this, their familiarity with the French language was a great asset. Anita took a pragmatic view of that dangerous practice:

> I could never accept that I should be killed for how I happened to be born and decided to give the Germans a better reason for killing me.

The sisters made an attempt to escape to France with forged French papers and false names. But, unfortunately, they didn't get very far and were apprehended on the railway platform. After spending time in an orphanage and in the Wrocław prison, they were "tried" and accused of counterfeiting, aiding the enemy, and attempting to escape. They were sentenced to a long stint in prison — but there was more: they were sent separately to one of the thousands of concentration camps.

The Cellist in the Women's Orchestra

Anita was put on a train to Auschwitz. A prison term would undoubtedly have been more comfortable. She arrived in December 1943 and survived the SS's notorious first selection, during which many newcomers were marched directly to the gas chambers. From one moment to the next, Anita became number 69388.

An attractive, well-dressed woman came into her barracks after she arrived. When the woman heard that

Anita played the cello, she told her that her life would be spared. The lady in question was Alma Rosé, Gustav Mahler's niece, a daughter of Mahler's sister. Alma Rosé's father had been the concertmaster of the Vienna Philharmonic, and she was an excellent violinist herself. In the camp, Alma Rosé had been drafted into the music department. Thanks to her name and reputation, she became the conductor of the women's orchestra, taking over from the previous conductor, who, curiously, was named Tchaikowska. After the war, Rosé was subject to harsh criticism because she had been named a *Kapo*; in other words, the enemy had made her a trustee inmate, and she hadn't demurred. She used her position to lead the orchestra with an iron fist. That wasn't always appreciated. On the other side of the coin, of course, her unrelenting attitude kept the minds of her musicians sharp. She ensured that their lives were spared by strictly maintaining the orchestra's artistic level. Anita acknowledged the positive side of that attitude throughout her life. She had no qualms, for example, about the time Alma forced her to scrub the floor on her knees for playing poorly.

For her audition, Anita played Franz Schubert's "Marche militaire." Although she hadn't touched her instrument in two years, her educational basis was so strong she was easily accepted into Auschwitz's *Mädchenorchester* (Women's Orchestra) as the only cellist. She was housed in a special barracks — block 12. There, Anita met two Belgian women: the violinist Hélène Scheps, born in the Swiss city of Basel, and Fanny Kornblum-Birkenwald, who played the mandolin. Fanny was later interviewed by Luckas Vander Taelen for a Belgian television documentary called *De laatste getuigen* (The last witnesses).

The orchestra, made up of some forty members, was by no stretch of the imagination a fully balanced symphonic ensemble. It made use of whatever musicians and instruments it could find. Most were neither professionally trained nor especially talented. Hélène, Fanny, and Anita are all mentioned in *Sursis pour l'orchestre*, a book written by their orchestral colleague the French pianist and cabaret artist Fania Fénelon. Her eyewitness account was later filmed as *Playing for Time*, with Vanessa Redgrave playing the role of Fania.

For various reasons, some survivors criticized both the book and the film. Squabbles couldn't be avoided from time to time, even within that downtrodden community. According to Anita, the biggest advantage of her new situation was that she was now recognized as "the cellist," not just another anonymous woman with a shaved head. Yet every day the musicians faced harsh realities. They owed the orchestra's existence, and their lives, to Maria Mandel, an SS officer nicknamed "the Beast." She was both a murdering Fräulein and a fanatical fan of music with a weakness for Giacomo

Puccini — such a cynical combination. She had founded the Auschwitz Women's Orchestra, and she was so taken with her pet project that she had block 12 custom built with a wooden floor and heating to protect the instruments. Orchestral life was centered there; it's where the musicians lived and rehearsed. The orchestra had a wide-ranging mission. They played for the prisoners in the morning, sometimes accompanying their work. They also performed on special occasions, such as visits from Nazi bigwigs. Sometimes they played privately for camp leaders, or when trains arrived with new detainees. One member of the orchestra, Esther Bejarano, remembered how they would play standing up when those convoys arrived. The newcomers would wave at them and smile, perhaps thinking that any place that gave them such a festive, musical welcome couldn't be that bad.

The Women's Orchestra had a limited repertoire. They didn't have much sheet music and had to make do with piano parts arranged on the spot and copied by hand for the instruments available to the orchestra. They otherwise relied on tunes the women could remember, which were then written down and arranged. This limited their repertoire to a mixture of light classical music and the day's popular tunes. Their programs included the "Csárdás" by Vittorio Monti, Pablo de Sarasate's "Zigeunerweisen" (Gypsy airs, an ironic title in such a camp), music by the pianist and composer Peter Kreuder,

"The Blue Danube" and other waltzes by Strauss, German marches and folk songs, and arias from popular opera such as *Rigoletto, Carmen,* and *Madame Butterfly.* *Schlager* music—a German genre of catchy, sentimental ballades—was also played. For instance, when Esther Bejarano auditioned on her accordion, she played "Du hast Glück bei den Frau'n, Bel Ami," a smash hit at that time first sung by Lizzi Waldmüller.

The orchestra declined after Alma Rosé's death, but it remained intact. One day in Auschwitz, Anita spotted her little sister, Renate. Their unexpected reunion gave each of them a much needed dose of fortitude during that horrendous period. Renate accompanied Anita when the Red Army approached the camp at the end of October 1944. The entire complex was hastily evacuated, and for six interminable months the sisters were housed in Bergen-Belsen. There, in the freezing cold, they huddled in a cramped tent with nothing but a thin blanket for warmth. During a storm, the tent collapsed, and they huddled together in the pouring rain, practically naked. Bergen-Belsen meant either dying of an illness such as typhus or simply perishing from hardship. The ordeal sometimes led to cannibalism, as when Anita witnessed a man munching on a human ear. She later said that it had been a miracle she survived, and she had her cello to thank. There was no place for an orchestra in Bergen-Belsen, but the solidarity among the orchestra members remained strong. The women looked out for one another and did what they could to keep morale high. They kept going. At one point the circumstances in the camp were so appalling that Anita and Renate decided to take matters into their own hands. They still had some cyanide tucked away, just in case, but when they swallowed it, it tasted like granulated sugar. They had had the poison with them in jail. Apparently, one of their fellow inmates had surreptitiously switched the tiny bags of white power with sugar to prevent them from making the ultimate bid for freedom. Yet another sort of miracle, but a mildly amusing one.

Gradually, certain rumors started making the rounds, and the sisters sensed a change in atmosphere; of course, there was no way of knowing if their release was genuinely imminent. But in April of 1945, salvation arrived. The soldiers were initially stunned and bewildered when they saw all that had happened. But the inmates were liberated. Anita and Renate recorded a message in a BBC truck, and back in England a friend of Marianne's heard it. They reestablished contact, and it was the start of an intense exchange of correspondence between the sisters. But the hardship was not yet at an end.

It took months before the entire camp was evacuated and everyone found a destination. They knew it was only a matter of time, which gave them courage and the strength to carry on. At times the living conditions bordered on luxury, as when one senior officer gave Anita the marvelous gift of a cello! In her letters to Marianne, the first thing Anita requested were étude books and the score of Bach's *Cello Suites* to practice and regain her former level of proficiency. In the meantime, she took every opportunity to enjoy her reclaimed freedom. She attended concerts given by the pacifist British composer and pianist Benjamin Britten and the Jewish violinist Yehudi Menuhin. She went to a performance of Mozart's *Marriage of Figaro*. Lady Montgomery, the British woman in charge of "entertainment," introduced Anita to some other musicians, including the cellist Giuseppe Selmi. They formed a chamber music ensemble and played in some of the other former camps.

Many years later, the English cellist Raphael Wall-fisch performed Schumann's Cello Concerto in Florence. There, he discovered that the orchestra's principal cellist was none other than Giuseppe Selmi. It was a heartfelt encounter, because Raphael is the son of Anita Lasker. After the evacuation of Bergen-Belsen and the trial of Lüneburg—at which Anita testified—she set her heart on living in England. But to get there, she first had to go to the British passport office in Brussels. For her, it was the start of a memorable interlude: for three months she lived in that free, lively, and vibrant city. She attended concerts, found a cello teacher to help her improve her rusty technique, joined the university's symphony orchestra, and generally basked in her freedom. Then, in March 1946, eleven months after being set free, Anita boarded a ship in Ostend on her way to a new life in England. After the long nightmare she had endured, her dream became a reality.

The Cellist of the Chamber Orchestra

She married Peter Wallfisch, another Jewish musician from Wrocław. He had escaped in time and had managed to avoid most of the miseries of war. Together with her husband and a few others, including Arnold Goldsborough, Anita set up the Goldsborough Orchestra in London. In 1960 the ensemble was renamed. It became the celebrated English Chamber Orchestra, where she continued to play for many years.

The Wallfisch-Laskers had two children. One is Raphael Wallfisch, who is still active on the concert circuit. His children also entered the field of music: Benjamin is a composer of film scores, Simon is a talented baritone, and Joanna is a singer-songwriter. What luck that Anita swallowed table sugar instead of the deadly alternative! She found a positive way of dealing with her incredible experiences and never stopped believing she would survive. Her goal was to pay back those bastards for what they'd done to her. In this she kept her word. She didn't insult Germans or go on the attack. Instead, in writings, interviews, and lectures, she warned future generations about the dangers of anti-Semitism and other forms of racism and intolerance. In January 2018 she spoke before the assembled German Bundestag.

When she was asked in an interview if she ever felt guilty for having survived while so many others had perished, she answered: "What do you think? What should I have said when they asked me to play in that *Mädchenorchester*? No, thank you, I only play in Carnegie Hall?"

There's that beautiful Jewish humor again. But does this mean all is forgotten? Far from it. One bitter detail from her time in the Women's Orchestra has remained etched in her memory: It was a performance for camp commanders, including the notorious Josef Mengele. She was forced to play Robert Schumann's tender *Träumerei*, especially for him. Afterward, she overheard one of the commanders say: *"Ein bewunderenswertes Stück, das geht ans Herz!"* (An admirable piece that touches the heart). Hard to imagine anything more sinister.

Paul Hindemith
The Atonal Noisemaker

The Hindemith case caused a lot of upheaval during those turbulent times, not the least because important figures were involved, one of whom was Paul Hindemith himself. This time, no physical suffering was involved, and no psychological despair. Instead, there was an intense clash between two opposing ideas about musical culture and cultural politics: those of the Third Reich and those of full-blooded musicians. Hindemith was all the more a "case" because his relationship with Nazism was paradoxical and considerably inconsistent. Goebbels himself once said that Hindemith was undeniably one of the leading talents among the German composers of the younger generation. And yet, Hindemith was forced to seek his salvation outside of Germany. How can these contradictions be reconciled?

Born in 1895 in Hanau near Frankfurt am Main, Hindemith was a uniquely multifaceted musician. He is primarily remembered as a composer, but he was much more than that. Hindemith was also a fine violinist.

When he was young, he played as deputy leader of the opera orchestra in Frankfurt. Shortly after that, he was promoted to concertmaster. Hindemith's career was briefly interrupted when he was drafted into the army during the First World War. He was stationed on the Flemish front as a sentry. But his real strength as a musician lies with another instrument, one he wholeheartedly embraced: he was undoubtedly one of the most important violists of his generation. He performed solo concerts worldwide and premiered numerous works, including William Walton's Viola Concerto. He played in various chamber music ensembles and founded the Amar Quartet. And, he achieved all this playing an instrument that is often the subject of ridicule.

Among musicians and music lovers, jokes about the viola abound. To give an idea: "How can you protect your violin from being stolen? Keep it in a viola case." The viola's dubious reputation may have to do with the difficulty of what is essentially a supporting instrument. In the wrong hands the viola can sound less brilliant, agile, and flamboyant than the violin. Players have to be highly skilled to reach any level of proficiency. Maybe that — and the primarily supportive role of their instrument — explains why violists can sometimes become frustrated or start to slack off. On the plus side, the viola's deeply warm sonority adds an essential dimension to both solo works and the overall sound of the orchestra. In his Octet, Hindemith wrote a breathtaking solo part for the viola, proving that the instrument should not be relegated to the background.

Hindemith was not just a composer and an instrumentalist. He was also a conductor, especially in his later career. He taught at prestigious institutions in Berlin, Turkey, the United States, and Switzerland. His gift for correspondence is perhaps less well known. The epistles he wrote to his wife during his many concert tours are gems of poetic and humorous charm, playful with, at times, biting criticism. They contain amusing outbursts about the world of music in general and specific colleagues in particular. They also provide some insight into Hindemith's stance concerning the political situation.

Hindemith had humble beginnings. In his youth he made ends meet playing the violin in cafés, dance orchestras, and theaters. Perhaps that is why he wrote so many pieces of *Gebrauchsmusik* or utility music. He composed for anyone who had a need. He produced works for the player piano, wrote music for children's games and for youth groups, hoping to heighten their sensitivity to beauty. He also wrote sonatas for nearly every wind instrument because the winds lacked repertoire. He composed works for amateur orchestras, test pieces for musical exams, and functional background music for radio plays. If he were alive today, Hindemith would likely be working for the gaming industry. Once, when he was a guest in Freiburg, he wrote to his wife: "During dinner I wrote seven short duos for his [Erich Dolflein's] violin school." That's typical Hindemith: idealism combined with "all in a day's work."

Breaking with the Past

Hindemith regularly conducted amateur choirs, and (now we're getting to the crux of the matter) he also contributed to political consciousness raising. He collaborated with Kurt Weill on the first version of the radio cantata, *Der Lindberghflug* (the Lindberg flight) by Bertolt Brecht, and he composed music for that same author's 1927 *Lehrstük* (Teaching play). Of course, such activities made Hindemith suspicious in certain right-wing circles; yet he may not have been motivated by political convictions. Perhaps he simply took these assignments on as work or because he had been asked. During his lessons at the Academy of Music, he didn't go beyond voicing some criticism of the regime. He was first and foremost a musician, although that didn't hold water with the right wing, who found his music galling.

Like many of his contemporaries, Hindemith wanted to break with past romanticism, a trend previously set in motion by the impressionists. He also sought more adventurous approaches. As a modernist, Hindemith wanted to go beyond the days of euphonious melodies and harmonies and the need for comfortable listening pleasure. He sought out forms of expression that were dynamic and surprising. He found them in his own seemingly boundless imagination as well as in the airy, often-humorous musical inventions of his contemporaries. During that period, classical composers picked up and adapted American jazz, cabaret melodies, and even sentimental pop songs. In his *Suite "1922,"* Hindemith unabashedly stylized the era's popular American dance rhythms, including the shimmy, the Boston, and a frenzied ragtime. He did not copy that music but wrapped it in his own musical language. Hindemith invented sharp, biting, rhythmic patterns and shrill, dissonant, out-of-tune-sounding chords that were challenging for classical music lovers. He flirted—nothing more than that—with atonality, a style that took dissonance a step further.

A piece of music is generally composed in a particular key so that all its notes sound "correct." But atonality does not take into account any fixed, continuing key signature. The notes may seem to be stuck together more or less randomly, as in a collage. This type of music lacks melodious, logical harmonies, and that's something some music lovers can only marginally appreciate. Such music, after all, does not appeal to a listener's natural appreciation of and longing for easily accessible beauty.

The Nazis, of course, took a dim view of any break with the past, but Hindemith never went as far as that. His music is not especially alienating, although listeners rarely left the concert hall humming the tune. For music critics with Nazi leanings, this was sufficient grounds for declaring Hindemith an iconoclast. At the end of the 1920s, they focused their wrath on him. They accused him of feeling at home in every genre except in the soul of German folk music. The critics completely overlooked Hindemith's sparkling humor, vitality, and inventiveness. Over time the Jewish issue also caught up with Hindemith. In 1929 Alfred Rosenberg in the *Völkischer Beobachter*, the Nazis' official newspaper, disparaged him for being "Jewish-connected." There was some truth to that: Hindemith's wife, Gertrud Rottenberg, was half-Jewish, the composer frequently played with Jewish musicians, and he had many Jewish friends. The Nazis gave him bad marks for that, as well.

Internationally, Hindemith's compositions attracted attention, and he was a welcome guest at various new music festivals. Perhaps that is why those in charge treated their cultural poster boy with kid gloves. However, in 1930 in Dresden, Hindemith's *Sancta Susanna*, a daring one-act opera, was canceled at the last minute, due to fears of disruption.

In Disgrace

When the Nazis ultimately assumed power in 1933, Hindemith's position became increasingly precarious. He was labeled the *Bannerträger des Verfalls* (standard-bearer of decay) because the regime viewed his music as "cultural Bolshevism." Nevertheless, Hindemith blithely continued playing in his trio with Jewish colleagues Simon Goldberg, violin, and Emanuel Feuermann, cello. He also played with Artur Schnabel and cellist Pablo Casals (Pau Casals I Defilló, in Catalan), a notorious anti-fascist. Gradually, Hindemith's wife, Gertrude, took on a more prominent role. He referred to her as Pushu, Herzenspushu of Leu in his letters, collected in *Das private Logbuch*.

Nevertheless, within the regime, specific figures continued to view Hindemith as the man of the future. At first he wasn't too worried. Recent developments didn't seem particularly unfavorable, because Hindemith tried not to take sides politically. He did his best to avoid confrontation. Some sources claim he even tried to get in the regime's good books, going so far as to invite Hitler to his composition class. While that may be true, there was no love lost between Hindemith and the new leader. Their relationship was doomed from the start. Hitler's dislike of Hindemith was simply too great. It dated from Hindemith's 1929 opera, *Neues vom Tage*, in which a naked soprano appeared onstage.

This sealed Hindemith's fate; things gradually deteriorated He fell out of favor in Germany, both as a performer and a composer. There was no official ban on performing his works, but concert organizers stopped programming them. When they tried, the artistic directors were often sacked immediately. Hindemith rarely mentioned the situation in his letters to his wife—and he hid nothing from her. If he did let anything slip, it was to say that he had little sympathy for colleagues who'd jumped on the Nazi bandwagon. In a letter from May 1933, he sneered cynically at the writer Gottfried Benn, who had joined the Nazi Party: "Purely for your amusement, I am sending you the latest speech by our hearth cricket, Jottfried [sic]. He's done well for himself....I'm looking forward to his disenchantment in a few months."

He lumped the world-famous pianist Wilhelm Backhaus in the same category: "Perhaps Benn will make it as far as Wilhelm Backhaus, who suddenly turned up from America, where he's known as William Bachhaus. On posters for his piano recital in Berlin are the words, 'At the request of the German Chancellor.' The Herr Chancellor has promised to attend." Backhaus was one of the most prominent pianists of his time. He met Hitler during a flight shortly after Hitler assumed power. The two became best friends, exchanging compliments and small presents. Backhaus became an advisor to the

Kameradschaft der deutschen Künstler (Fellowship of German Artists). Hitler granted him the title of "Professor" and invited him to be his personal guest at Nuremberg for the *Reichsparteitag*. Hindemith also ridiculed the pianist for sometimes spelling his name *Bach*aus, as if riding on the coattails of the great Johann Sebastian Bach.

In March 1934 the Hindemith case came to a head because of his opera *Mathis der Maler*. The piece revolved around Matthias Grünewald, a sixteenth-century painter whose given name was Mathis. (Grünewald's most celebrated work, the *Isenheim Altarpiece*, is on display in the Unterlinden Museum in Colmar, France.) To many, Hindemith's work expresses political solidarity with the poor and oppressed. Before the completed opera was premiered, Hindemith presented the public with a three-movement symphony, a piece for the concert stage based on musical fragments of material later reworked for the opera. On the night of the premiere, Wilhelm Furtwängler conducted the orchestra. For that symphonic work, Hindemith had used a slightly more accessible musical language, either intentionally, by chance, or simply because the work dealt with a historical theme. Compared with some of his earlier works, *Mathis de Maler* sounded more traditional, warmer, more good-natured, and classical. This did not go unnoticed by the critic Friedrich Wilhelm Herzog. In his review, he called Hindemith an ingenious musician, and he said that although the music of the symphony was contemporary, it still had a link with the past. Bygone norms and values were of great importance to the Nazis. Add the work's historical Germanic subject matter to the mix, and things for the composer were looking pretty rosy. Hindemith was able to complete his opera in peace. Unfortunately, interest in his other works also died down; they were hardly played any longer. His opponents kept trying to push him into obscurity. Until Herzog, in the magazine *Das Musik zu Wort*, launched a head-on attack on Hindemith. His previous praise for the symphony had been replaced by earlier arguments.

Frivolous, Rudderless, and Idiosyncratic

New music, particularly by Hindemith, was seen as anti-romantic and an apparent attack on Wagner. The Nazis viewed Wagner as their musical god. Yet Hindemith gave Grünewald's hellish demons an infernal and apocalyptic sound. This was a far cry from the hearty Germanic music the regime and its sympathizers had been expecting. It didn't help that Grünewald, like Hindemith, had also been married to a Jewish woman. Wilhelm Furtwängler, who had been slated to conduct the opera's premiere, sprang to Hindemith's defense. Although Furtwängler wasn't a Nazi and regularly voiced his disapproval, between 1922 and 1945 he

was the chief conductor of the Berlin Philharmonic—
yet another figure the Nazis didn't dare touch because
he was well known and popular, both nationally and
internationally.

In November 1934 Furtwängler published an opinion piece in the *Deutsche Allgemeine Zeitung*. He stood
up for Hindemith, which marked the beginning of the
Furtwängler-Goebbels controversy. Goebbels retaliated
in early December in a speech before the Reichskulturkammer. He called Hindemith "an atonal noisemaker"
and "spiritually un-Aryan." He used other bon mots
such as "frivolous," "rudderless," and "idiosyncratic."
Hindemith was clearly not one to march in step with the
Nazis or anyone else. He was beyond purely political content and opinions about art, aesthetics, and the state's
role therein. There were immediate protests against the
performance of the opera, which was to have taken place
in Berlin. The Nazis forbade the production. Goebbels
was clear: "National Socialism is not only the political
and social conscience but also the cultural conscience of
the nation."

Hindemith hardened his stance and spoke openly
against every form of fascism, both in the arena of personal life and in politics and culture. He saw the storm
clouds gathering, and so, on the day before Goebbels
was to make his speech, he asked the director of the Berlin Musikhochschule (Music Academy), where he then

taught, to grant him indefinite leave. Furtwängler was forced to step down from the Berlin State Opera because of his actions, but he was later reinstated, with his tail between his legs.

Hindemith left Germany and continued his musical and pedagogical activities elsewhere. He moved to Turkey, where he set up a conservatory of music based on Western European models. He also resided in Switzerland, and it was there, in Zürich, that his opera *Mathis der Maler* was finally premiered in May 1938. He emigrated to the United States from Switzerland and became an American citizen in 1946. His final years were devoted to teaching and composing. In the United States he joined the faculty of Yale University. When he returned to Europe in 1953, he taught at the University of Zürich, the city that had premiered his opera. Hindemith, who no longer played the viola, died in Frankfurt in 1963.

Fritz Löhner-Beda
The Hit Machine

"It wouldn't hurt that Jewish swine to work a little harder!" This casual remark, made by an SS officer in Auschwitz, led to the death of Fritz Löhner-Beda. Never heard of Löhner-Beda? His name may not ring a bell, but in his day (1883–1942), the man was well-known in the world of German-language popular music and light classics.

He was a lyricist, but he also made a significant musical contribution to the creation of innumerable compositions. His list of works includes many hits, such as "Du schwarzer Zigeuner" (You black Gypsy), "Oh, Donna Clara," "Ausgerechnet Bananen" (Of all things bananas, an adaptation of "Yes! We Have No Bananas," once sung by Josephine Baker), "Gern hab' ich die Frau'n geküsst" (I like to kiss the women), "Ich hab' mein Herz in Heidelberg verloren" (I lost my heart in Heidelberg), "Dein ist mein ganzes Herz" (My whole heart is yours, immortalized by tenor Richard Tauber), "Meine Lippen, sie küssen so heiß" (My lips, they kiss so hot), and "Freunde,

das Leben ist lebenswert" (Friends, life is worth living). He also wrote the librettos of successful operettas by Franz Lehár and Paul Abraham, including *Friederike* (Frederica), *Das Land des Lächelns* (The land of smiles), *Viktoria und ihr Husar* (*Victoria and Her Hussar*), *Die Blume von Hawaii* (The flower of Hawaii), and *Ball im Savoy* (*Ball at the Savoy*). These were major international hits for decades, both in the original German and in other languages. The practice of translating popular songs into almost every language continued until late in the 1950s. A great deal of the hits mentioned above are undoubtedly still fresh in the minds of readers who were born or grew up in that era.

In 1974 the Greek singer Vicky Leandros revived one of Löhner-Beda's texts, "Rosa wir fahr'n nach Lodz" (Rosa, we're going to Lodz). She turned Rosa into Theo and climbed the western European charts with that number, which was later popular in America as "Henry, Let's Go to Town," and in Britain as "Danny, Teach Me to Dance." Interesting to note that the Rosa from the 1915 original was, in fact, a cannon. Löhner-Beda had served as an officer in the First World War, an experience that turned him into a pacifist for life.

In 1910, after studying law (he worked for a time in an attorney's office), Löhner-Beda began a career as a free-lance writer. Using various pen names, he wrote texts for almost every genre: newspaper articles, satire, song lyrics, and material for cabaret. His meeting with Franz Lehár in 1913 proved a turning point; Lehár brought him into contact with operetta, which was then immensely popular. Being associated with a composer of Lehár's stature meant that Löhner-Beda had truly hit the big time. From that day onward, Löhner-Beda focused primarily on song texts. He was, incidentally, a man of many talents. In addition to his writing abilities, he was a gifted soccer player. And in 1934 he became vice president of the Society of Austrian Authors, Composers, and Publishers, comparable with ASCAP in the United States. In short, Löhner was a man to be reckoned with.

His family sensed the impending threat early on. When Fritz was still a child, they moved to Vienna from their home in what is now the Czech Republic. Once in Vienna they changed their family name from Löwy to Löhner. While the two are similar, Löhner sounds more German (and less Jewish). Bedrich's Slavic first name was also Germanized, and he later added the shortened form of Bedrich—Beda—to his surname.

He Died because Franz Lehár Forgot Him

Although Löhner-Beda openly criticized the Nazis from the start, he wasn't particularly worried about the regime. He once said, "Hitler loves my songs!" Sadly, that wasn't enough to protect him; on 13 March 1938, one day after the Anschluss, he was rounded up with the *Prominententransport* and sent to Dachau. Before the Wehrmacht invaded Austria on 12 March, German officers flew to Austria and started arresting politicians, officials, socialists, communists, and other potential opponents of the regime, removing "prominent" enemies; Löhner-Beda was one. Apparently, Hitler's clemency for Lehár did not extend to his most important lyricist. Not in Dachau, not in Buchenwald, and ultimately, not in Auschwitz. In an ironic twist of fate, during Löhner-Beda's initial period of imprisonment, a gala performance was given in Vienna featuring Lehár's operetta *Das Land des Lächelns,* and many high-ranking Nazis were in the audience. More ironic still is that during that same period, Löhner-Beda, together with his friend, the actor/singer/cabaret artist Fritz Grünbaum, was putting on small-scale performances in the camp, singing many of his own songs.

It seems that Lehár, the operetta king, didn't lift a finger to save Fritz from certain death. There were later claims from Lehár's corner that he had done everything he could, although after the war Lehár claimed he never even knew his former friend had been imprisoned. An incomplete recollection? Or a fabrication?! That almost rhymes. Löhner-Beda wrote to Lehár from the camp, pleading for help. Lehár replied that he had done what he could: he'd have the Führer look into the case, although no proof of such an exchange can be found. Viktor Matejka, the progressive Catholic communist writer and cultural politician who survived the hell of the camps, later proclaimed: "Löhner had to die because Lehár had forgotten about him." Löhner-Beda himself held onto the belief that Lehár would intervene on his behalf. He remained optimistic for a long time. One of the camp poems he wrote in Buchenwald gives an indication of his positive attitude:

> *Doch mich schlägt kein Tiger, mich frisst kein Hai,*
> *Der Tod geht täglich an mir vorbei.*
> *An mir beißt der Teufel die Zähne sich aus,*
> *Ich fühl'es Ich komm' aus der Hölle heraus,*
> *Ich warte.*

> But no tiger beats me, no shark eats me,
> Every day, Death passes me by.
> The devil sinks his teeth in me,
> I feel like I'm coming out of hell,
> I wait.

The Löhner-Beda family was left behind when he was captured. His eldest child, Bruno, from his first marriage with Anni Akselradi, did manage to emigrate to the United States. His second wife was Helene Jelline, to whom he dedicated his "Dein ist mein ganzes Herz." He signed over Villa Felicitas, a house he owned in Bad

Ischl, to her. After he was arrested, Helene was gradually stripped of all her possessions. In the summer of 1942 she was sent to Minsk with their two daughters, Liselotte, aged thirteen, and Evamaria, fourteen. All three were gassed in the Maly Trostinets death camp. But Fritz Löhner-Beda never knew of their fate. Prior to their arrest, they regularly sent him letters and money. In the camp poem mentioned earlier, he asked himself what had happened to them:

Das Weib und die Kinder, die sitzen zu Haus,
Bald sind es fünf Jahre! Wie sehen sie wohl aus?
Ich sehe die grosse verdunkelte Stadt,
Da sinds sie verkrochen und werden nicht satt,
Und warten.

My wife and the children, who sit in the house
It's been almost five years. What do they look like now?
I see the big city in darkness,
there they hide, always hungry,
And wait.

Half a year after being imprisoned in Dachau, he was sent to Buchenwald. As soon as he arrived, the camp commander began a competition for a camp hymn. Fritz, a born lyricist, couldn't resist such a chance. His Jewish fellow prisoner Hermann Leopoldi provided the music, and they won. But because the two were Jewish, the winning hymn was released under the name of a German camp leader, along with the promise that they would be compensated later. It goes without saying that they never received their prize. However, when American troops liberated the camp, the surviving detainees sang the winning "Song of Buchenwald":

When the day awakes, before the sun laughs, the crew
embark for the toils of the day,
into the dawn.
And the forest is black and the sky red,
we carry a small piece of bread in our bags,
    and in our hearts,
our sorrows.
Oh Buchenwald, I cannot forget you,
    because you are my fate.
Only one who has left you, can measure,
how wonderful freedom is!
Oh, Buchenwald, we neither lament, nor complain,
and whatever our future may hold:
we still want to say "yes" to life,
because one day the time will come —
then we will be free!
Our blood runs hot and the girl is far,
and the wind sings softly, and I love her dearly,
If she's true, remains true to me!

The stones are hard, but our steps determined,
and we carry the picks and spades with us,
And in our hearts, our hearts love.
    (Refrain.)
The night is so short and the days so long,
But if a song from our homeland is heard,
we do not let it rob us of our courage.
Keep pace, comrade, and do not lose courage
for we carry the will to live in our blood
and in our hearts, our hearts of faith.

Typical Fritz Löhner-Beda lyrics — fully aware of the hell into which he had descended, maintaining hope for the future, and staying strong with a smattering of (Jewish?) humor. For a year and a half, Karl Schnog, one of Löhner-Beda's fellow prisoners, sat beside him at the table. One morning, someone tried to point out the beauty of the dawn. Fritz shot back, "Good friend, I have seen enough sunrises to last me ten years!" When another inmate grumbled that life could become even bleaker for them in the future, he answered: "How can vinegar become more bitter?" One night after work, one of his songs blared through the camp radio. When it was over, he bowed to the radio and said, "The author would like to express his gratitude." Of course, the names of the Jewish composers and lyricists were not announced. Löhner-Beda didn't write many more song lyrics in

Buchenwald; there was work to be done. At first, he was assigned to the sock-darning crew. Later, he was transferred to a gardening detail.

Buchenwald was only a way station. On 17 October 1942, Löhner-Beda was transferred to KZ Auschwitz III Monowitz, to work for IG Farben. That company, a cornerstone of Hitler's empire, had been founded partly by Carl Bosch—from the family that manufactures electrical appliances. During the Nazi era, IG Farben had a near monopoly on everything produced in the way of chemicals. In Auschwitz III, Löhner-Beda was a forced laborer assigned to build IG Farben's new Buna plant producing synthetic rubber. Löhner-Beda is also said to have written words to a Buna hymn. But after only a few weeks, he started showing severe signs of deterioration; that didn't escape the notice of the camp's commanders. It's almost certain that Löhner-Beda died on 4 December, and the exact circumstances are also known. Some reports mention starvation and others gassing, but the most reliable comes from the testimony of a fellow prisoner named Raymond van den Straaten. His version was cited during the trials held against IG Farben. The minutes state: "One day two Buna prisoners, the Herr Raymond van den Straaten and the Herr Fritz Löhner-Beda, were on their way to work when a group of IG Farben bigwigs passed by. One of the directors pointed to Herr Löhner-Beda and said to the SS guard accompanying him: "That Jewish swine could stand to work a little harder." Then, another IG Farben director said: "When they can't work anymore, they should be snuffed out in the gas chamber."

After the delegation had passed, Herr Löhner-Beda was taken out of his work detail, beaten, and kicked. He returned to his friend in camp, barely alive. His life at the IG Farben plant in Auschwitz was over. Löhner-Beda's fatal beating was also described by the scholar and academic Raul Hilberg in his book *The Destruction of the European Jews*. The *Kapo* was cleared of the murder during the 1968 Auschwitz Trial, due to lack of evidence. *Freunde, das Leben ist lebenswert!* (Friends, we should still say "yes" to life!)

Willem Mengelberg
National Hero

In 2009 two recordings were found in a secondhand book-store in Lyon. They were from a wartime broadcast by pro-German Radio Paris of a concert held in the Théâtre des Champs-Elysées. No one knows how the recordings ended up in Lyon. During the war, the orchestra from Radio Paris was the only one still playing. All the other Parisian orchestras had been disbanded, so Radio Paris was free to recruit the best of the unemployed musicians, forming a world-class ensemble. Organizing prestigious concerts was the radio network's way of disguising its pro-German sympathies while showing how peaceful and culturally minded the occupiers were. The concerts were free and open to all: well-behaved French citizens sat shoulder to shoulder with polite German officers. The occupying forces also garnered support with their choice of the programs: the orchestra played a symphony by the Belgian composer César Franck; the Piano Concerto in F Minor by the Francophile Pole Frédéric Chopin; the *Pathetique Symphony* by the Russian *Untermensch*

Peter Tchaikovsky; and a Cello Concerto by another Slav, Antonin Dvořák. What had happened to the racial issue? On the radio, people at home could enjoy cultural events featuring contributions from the most important figures of their day. In that radio recording from Paris, it was the great Dutch conductor Willem Mengelberg. That was no coincidence.

Mengelberg was born to German parents in 1871 in the Dutch city of Utrecht. His father, Friedrich Wilhelm, was an architect who specialized in religious buildings. His mother, Helena Schrattenholz, was a pianist who fed Willem breast milk sweetened with nuts. After Willem Mengelberg completed his studies of piano and orchestral conducting at the Cologne Conservatory, he went to Lucerne in 1892 to become the city's general music director or *Städtischer Musikdirektor*. A talented young musician, Mengelberg was chosen from among hundreds of candidates, although in a letter to his parents, he boasted that "more than two hundred" had vied for the position. Typical Mengelberg. In a sleepy city like Lucerne, the job of general music director was anything but prestigious. He had to conduct the municipal orchestra's subscription concerts, and he was in charge of three choirs. In addition, he ran the local music school. It was a modest position in a small Swiss city, but it was an ideal place for Mengelberg to learn his trade through trial and error.

His progress was so exemplary that when Willem

Kes, the then chief conductor of Amsterdam's Concert-gebouw Orchestra, was lured to Glasgow, Scotland, by higher fees, Mengelberg's name cropped up as a replacement. Mengelberg, just twenty-four, was handed the job of principal conductor. At that time, the Concertgebouw Orchestra was nothing special, and to give credit where credit is due, Mengelberg quickly turned it into one of the best in the world.

He soon evolved into something of a national hero. He initiated the Dutch practice of performing Bach's *St. Matthew Passion* every spring, a tradition that continues to this day. He also lured the greatest composers of the era to Amsterdam, including Gustav Mahler, Igor Stravinsky, and Richard Strauss. He joined forces with Amsterdam's Toonkunst Choir to present inexpensive popular concerts in the Paleis voor Volksvlijt, the Palace of People's Work. That Dutch crystal palace burned to the ground in 1929. The first of those concerts was held in 1904, and audience members paid the equivalent of a quarter to attend. This earned him the admiration of average working-class men and women. Nevertheless, Mengelberg is primarily remembered as the man who brought the orchestra to extraordinary heights, putting the Netherlands on the musical map. His reputation was on par with that of Arturo Toscanini, Bruno Walter, or Wilhelm Furtwängler. Between 1922 and 1930, he was the music director of the New York Philharmonic Orchestra.

In terms of widespread admiration, a survey in the Dutch magazine *Het Leven* ranked him just beneath Queen Wilhelmina. A classical musician becoming a national hero is pretty unique.

Delusions of Grandeur

Mengelberg probably reached his artistic pinnacle during the 1920 Mahler Festival, organized to celebrate his twenty-fifth anniversary as conductor of the Concertgebouw Orchestra. The festival presented two full weeks during which almost all of Mahler's works were performed. The stage was decorated with flowers and busts. Lectures, speeches, and celebrations commemorated Mahler's visits to Amsterdam as a guest conductor. In short, the event had international allure.

Gradually, however, and for various reasons, cracks began to appear in Mengelberg's angelic reputation. First, he got into hot water with the Dutch tax and customs administrations for failing to declare his foreign income. Then he moved to Switzerland, where he grumbled about insufficient appreciation in the Netherlands despite his lofty status. He was made an extraordinary professor at the University of Utrecht, but even this didn't improve his mood. He was clearly suffering from delusions of grandeur. And worst of all, the orchestra turned against him. After the highs of the 1920 Mahler Festival,

Mengelberg's relationship with the musicians gradually deteriorated. By 1935 the musicians had had enough of him. They no longer accepted his authoritarian manner, as one anecdote from that time demonstrates. When Mengelberg wouldn't stop reprimanding a horn player, the musician replied with the historic words, "Mr. Mengelenberg [intentionally mispronounced], *de pokke!*" Meaning roughly: "Drop dead." Admittedly, Mengelberg wasn't the only tyrannical conductor of that time. Most lorded it over the instrument-wielding peasants like all-knowing, all-important dictators.

Mengelberg grew more and more frustrated. He saw the rise of the German Reich and may have imagined it would give him a chance — both in the Netherlands and beyond — to elbow his way to the top. His German ancestry may have been a factor, along with his great love of Germanic music, although in this he was not alone. Some of his ill-considered activities and statements boomeranged back at him. For instance, when Adolf Hitler assumed power, Mengelberg was on tour in Germany. Without missing a step, he continued conducting. This was the first stain on his Dutch image. As a matter of fact, unlike Toscanini, Mengelberg remained active in Germany throughout the war. In Leipzig in November 1936, a statue of Felix Mendelssohn, the nineteenth-century romantic composer of Jewish birth, was torn down. When the press asked Mengelberg about the incident, he responded, "Gentlemen, don't believe those reports!" Yet they were true. The statue was never found and had probably been melted down for the war effort.

Mengelberg's career drifted along in relative calm until, in July 1940, an interview with him appeared in the *Völkischer Beobachter*, the Nazi newspaper. He said he'd uncorked the champagne and raised a glass to that *großartige Stunde*, that great hour when the Netherlands had capitulated. A few days later, when a translation of that interview appeared in Dutch newspaper *De Telegraaf*, Mengelberg was utterly disgraced. He tried to save face with the classic tale that the journalist had made it all up, but then he gave the game away by adding, "Why should I be vilified for voicing my sympathy for Germany?"

His allegiance didn't stop with words. On 1 May 1942 —International Workers' Day—Arthur Seyss-Inquart, the Austrian Nazi appointed by the Germans as Reich Commissioner of the Netherlands, was ordered to set up a Dutch labor front. It was intended to replace all the existing Dutch labor unions and promote the Nazification of Dutch businesses, allowing them to fight against the Allies. Henk Woudenberg of the NSB—the Dutch National Socialist Movement, a Nazi political party— was put in charge. The union also had a cultural wing, called Vreugde en Arbeid (Joy and Labor), to rally popular support. Obviously, Jewish people were excluded.

Mengelberg was Vreugde en Arbeid's ideal promoter, thanks to his concerts for the common folk, and he gave many concerts for the movement. Photographs showing Mengelberg smiling beside Seyss-Inquart did nothing for Mengelberg's reputation.

Culture with a Capital K

During that same period, the Dutch NSB set up the Culture Council led by SS officer Geerto Snijder. They insisted on writing the Dutch word *Cultuur* with a *K*—contrary to the rules of Dutch spelling—to emphasize the familiar bond between the Germans and the Dutch. The Culture Council had twenty-two members, including two musicians: the composer Henk Badings and Willem Mengelberg. The council's assignment was to maintain control of the cultural life in the Netherlands and to assume the rightful positions owed them because of their origin and standing. To achieve this, they used their nature, strength, and above all, resolute goodwill. The activities of the Netherlands Culture Council (the *K* came later) were based on the conviction that a new order and a new rhythm were emerging in Europe. At first, the chairman listened to the advice of the board members, but later he made up his own mind, following the principles of the new regime.

(Interestingly, Mengelberg's agent was Rudolf Vedder,

a powerful concert impresario in Nazi Germany who represented almost all the great conductors of the time and who was also a close friend of Hermann Göring, although he sometimes had to lie low because of shady dealings.)

After the war, when the Dutch Central Board of Honor for the Arts looked into the Mengelberg case, their findings were harsh. They did not take the circumstances surrounding his actions into account, nor did they accept that he was no confirmed Nazi but, rather, a selfish, opportunistic, and somewhat naïve artist. They weren't impressed by Mengelberg's attempts to resist making the Concertgebouw Orchestra's repertoire more Aryan. It is true that, even after the German invasion, he continued to perform the work of his Jewish friend Gustav Mahler. He never stopped inviting Jewish musicians or musicians sympathetic to Jewish causes for guest appearances, including violinists Joseph Szigeti and Yehudi Menuhin, the pianist/composer Béla Bartók, and Mengelberg's conducting colleague Bruno Walter. He also continued to include composers and performers whose music was not in line with the aesthetic ideals of the Nazi Party, such as Paul Hindemith, the "atonal noisemaker." It's said that Mengelberg personally tried to intervene with Seyss-Inquart to prevent the dismissal of sixteen Jewish orchestra members.

One former Concertgebouw musician, Max Tak, a

great and multitalented Dutch musician, once wrote a letter to the maestro that could be used in Mengelberg's defense. Tak was able to escape the Netherlands, but the rest of his family died in German concentration camps. He sent a New Year's card to Mengelberg, concluding with, "please be assured that many are thinking of you, including your Max Tak, who was once honored by Willem Mengelberg's permission to play in his orchestra." But to the Central Board of Honor for the Arts, even these arguments in Mengelberg's favor fell on deaf ears. Accusations persisted of his having performed for high-ranking Nazis, refusing to perform music by Jewish composers (except Mahler), and not raising a finger when Jewish musicians were fired from his orchestra. In the end, the Central Board of Honor for the Arts permanently banned Mengelberg from conducting in the Netherlands, saying that the man should "never touch his conductor's baton" again. The verdict was later appealed, and the sentence reduced to six years, or until 1951. No one can be sure if Mengelberg ever considered returning to the concert stage, although it seems likely. He died in 1951 in Zuort, Switzerland, having never conducted another orchestra.

As is often the case, there are various reasons and different versions to explain why. And even if one version presents the correct facts, people form their own opinions based on their attitudes and convictions. At least, that's true in the Mengelberg case. His life has been studied, biographies have been written, and the Mengelberg Society tries to put everything into perspective. Today, it is more or less agreed that he was not a fervent Nazi, although he was a sympathizer, blinded mainly by his own hunger for glory. This last is also cited to explain why he was punished more severely than others who had more to answer for. In the end, his exemplary role as a national hero brought him more harm than good.

Franz Lehár
Idolized by Hitler

When Johann Strauss II died in 1899, fans of music and operetta feared it meant the end of their favorite genre. Nobody could take the place of such a genius, that much was clear. But behold: a new generation of musicians emerged who would carry on with that oh-so-distinct form of musical theater and at an equally high level. These musicians created a silver age to follow the golden one. Their uncontested standard-bearer was an Austrian of Hungarian descent called Franz Lehár. Or more correctly, Léhar Ferenc – because Hungarians usually place their surnames first. He was born in Komárom, situated in present-day Slovakia, now known as Komárno. Lehár studied music from the age of twelve at the Prague Conservatory, with the hope of becoming a classical violinist. There, the great composer Antonin Dvorak examined Lehár's earliest compositions. He noticed a remarkable talent and suggested Lehár concentrate on composing. Lehár took that advice to heart.

First, however, he decided to try and make it as a

violinist, perhaps out of necessity; money was tight. A beginning composer needs time to create, find an audience, and wait to see if their music catches on. And so Lehár became a violinist in the municipal Theatre Orchestra of Barmen-Elberfeld, now part of the German city of Wuppertal. After leaving that position, he followed in his father's footsteps and began working in various military bands: in the Hungarian city of Losonez (now the Croatian Pula), Trieste, and ultimately, Vienna. When Lehár's regiment was transferred, Lehár decided to stay behind in the era's foremost city for music and operetta. And with good reason: he had been hired to conduct the Theater an der Wien. Mozart, Beethoven, and Strauss had all triumphed in that iconic temple. There was no better place for Lehár to kick off his new career. He had composed a few pieces along the way, and now, under the very best circumstances, he could reveal his efforts to the world.

In 1902 his first operetta, *Wiener Frauen*, was premiered. His breakthrough, however, came in December 1905 with *Die lustige Witwe* (*The Merry Widow*). It was followed by such hits as *Paganini*, *The Count of Luxembourg*, *Der Zarewitsch* (*The Tzarevich*), and *The Land of Smiles*. The operettas were successful in their entirety, along with dozens of individual popular songs and duets excerpted from them. Lehár's ingenious melodies took on a life of their own, circling the globe with lyrics translated into numerous languages, as was the custom at the time. The plots were almost universally set in the Austro-Hungarian Empire, often featuring Roma people or characters from exotic locales. The lead characters were often wealthy members of the nobility, and the action was driven by ambiguous love relationships and saucy plot twists hinting at adultery. All topped off with copious amounts of liquor, preferably sparkling Sekt, champagne, or Tokay wine. Fashionable dances of that time—from the waltz to the cancan to swing and the czardas—were, of course, included.

Lehár savored his success; he was recognized everywhere he went and was surrounded by a flourishing business empire, making him incredibly wealthy. But then Nazism reared its ugly head. In the early years of the Third Reich, operettas by Lehár and others were regularly staged. Yet, by July 1933, a Berlin newspaper reported that Lehár's music was no longer being broadcast on the radio because of his criticism of the regime. In 1934 the Reich's dramaturge Rainer Schlösser wrote in a letter to Goebbels: "At the time of the assumption of power, the state of affairs in the operetta world was such that 80 percent of the work—both musically and in terms of lyrics—was of Jewish origin. Ten percent came from Aryan composers, but they also worked with Jewish librettists. Perhaps fewer than ten percent of the works were purely Aryan."

In November the Nazi ideologist Alfred Rosenberg echoed the "official" line: "Franz Lehár is a problem for the cultural politics of the Third Reich....Between his Jewish collaborators and Richard Tauber, he moves exclusively in Jewish circles in Vienna....Lehár's operettas are constructed according to an international pattern of kitsch. The lyrics set to music by him lack all German sentiment because they are produced by Jews. Lehár has excluded himself from the circle of contributors to the cultural politics of the Third. Reich." And indeed, almost all of Lehár's librettists were Jewish: Leo Stein, Victor Leon, Paul Knepler, Bela Jenbach, Alfred Grünwald, Julius Bauer, and above all, Fritz Löhner-Beda, whose harrowing tale was recounted earlier.

Rosenberg continued: "His wife...is reported to be Jewish. Lehár has proven his Aryan heritage. And yet, performing his works is unacceptable within the Nazi cultural movement." Rosenberg not only accused Lehár of moving in Jewish circles in Vienna, he also mentioned some sneering remarks Lehár is reported to have made about the cultural policies of the Nazis. Rosenberg may be referring to Lehár's 1934 operetta, *Giuditta*, seen by some — for reasons that escape me — as an attack on the Führer Principle. *Giuditta* was Lehár's last large-scale work. The French-language version of *Giuditta* was performed in 1935 in the Royal Theater of La Monnaie in Brussels, Belgium, in the composer's presence. Rosenberg did not pull any punches: "With all this, Lehár has made his position impossible within the cultural life of the Third Reich."

But there was a fairly serious problem. Because who should be Lehár's all-time greatest fan but Adolf Hitler? Followed closely by Joseph Goebbels! To Hitler, *The Merry Widow* was equal to the finest opera. Hitler's nearly morbid fascination with the work dated from its premiere in Vienna. The young Hitler had been enchanted not only by the music but by the subject matter. His housekeeper once caught him standing in front of the mirror, asking if he resembled the operetta's male lead, "Well? Am I not a genuine Danilo?" Rumor has it that *The Merry Widow* was the only thing Hitler would listen to in the final years of the war. How is one to make sense of such contradictions? Nazi leaders were crazy about operetta, but it was a musical genre dominated by Jewish librettists and composers. Well, the Nazis had ways of getting around such problems.

In the middle of the nineteenth century Jacques Offenbach, a German Jew, had become French, and the Nazis simply shunned him. Johann Strauss also had Jewish ancestry, but the Nazis didn't dare ban his music because he was immensely popular. Instead, they did everything they could to cover up Strauss's lineage. For Lehár the Nazis devised a different approach. Goebbels would personally make sure that the Führer could continue to enjoy his *Merry Widow*, along with the rest of Lehár's music, without suffering any loss of face. Goebbels had the librettos "revised" by Aryan lyricists, and the original authors' names were simply omitted.

Mrs. Lehár, Sophie Paschkis, was another problem. Before her marriage, she had converted to Catholicism, but she had initially been Jewish. For a time she had faced the threat of arrest and deportation. Finally, Goebbels intervened, and she was promoted to the status of honorary Aryan, or *Ehrenarier*, thus shielding her from harm. Lehár's name was, of course, taken off the boycott list. However, his major competitors (or their music, if they were no longer alive) remained verboten: Jacques Offenbach, Oscar Straus, Emmerich Kàlmàn, and Paul Abraham. One of the few Aryans among that group, Robert Stolz, refused to live in a country controlled by the Nazis and left. This meant that Lehár was the only undisputed operetta champion remaining, and Hitler could listen to his heart's content without compromising himself in the eyes of his supporters. The two men sometimes were even known to exchange gifts. Lehár gave Hitler a signed program book bound in red leather from the 1905 premiere of *The Merry Widow*. In a strange twist of fate the man who had sung the lead, Louis Treumann, was murdered along with his wife in Theresienstadt at almost the exact moment Lehár handed Hitler that gift. In

1940 the Führer awarded Lehár a Goethe Medal for Art and Science.

Serious or Decadent Music?

In 1938 this ambiguous state of affairs led to a high-level incident. At the famous exposition of "degenerate art" in Düsseldorf, Richard Strauss asked the organizer, Hans Ziegler, an awkward question. Strauss was no fan of government interference in artistic affairs (extra points for him) and half-jokingly wondered why neither his "atonal Salome" nor Franz Lehár's "decadent operettas" had been included in the exhibition. The answer was obvious: Adolf Hitler was a fan! But Richard Strauss's repeated grumblings about Lehár's operettas rankled. In the end Goebbels himself invited Strauss in for a chat, and later described that meeting in his diary: "I said a few nice things about his cheeky letters. He cannot stop writing those letters, and it's already brought him so much misery."

The composer Werner Egk was also at that meeting, and he noted in his memoirs that Goebbels had screamed and shouted: "Lehár draws the crowds; you don't! So you must stop talking about the importance of 'serious music.' You are not doing yourself any favors! Tomorrow's culture is different from yesterday's! You, Mr. Strauss, are from yesterday!" Clearly, the masses preferred Lehár to serious music. Therefore, the Nazi leaders unconditionally took Lehár's side.

In an ironic coincidence, when German troops marched into Vienna, they passed the Vienna State Opera where a poster announced *The Land of Smiles*, although the performances had been canceled. It was to have been a series of galas arranged by the Führer in honor of Lehár's seventieth birthday. Not much later, Bela Jenbach, one of Lehár's closest collaborators, died of starvation in Vienna. Lehár made no attempt to help him. In fact, he was by that time past his creative peak and would no longer produce anything of merit.

How did Lehár deal with all the conniving going on around him? He can't be labeled a confirmed anti-Semite, because of his marriage and his intense collaboration with Jewish artists like Richard Tauber and with his librettists. In fact, Richard Tauber tried to persuade Lehár to leave the country, as many others had done, but Lehár brushed off the suggestion. He had no desire at his age to end up in some unfamiliar country. However, he could have made such a move without risking his popularity, as Robert Stolz had done. Instead, he chose to bask in the protection of the ruling powers. He jumped at the chance to conduct a propaganda concert in Paris, had no trouble having his librettos Aryanized, made appearances at Nazi events, and dedicated his duet, *Lippen schweigen*, to the Führer. He even tried to dedicate his operetta *Giuditta* to Mussolini, but Il Duce turned him down; the work's fascist ideals were not sufficiently explicit. What's more, Lehár did little to save his Jewish associates and colleagues (see Fritz Löhner-Beda). Equally despicable was Lehár's active role in an extortion case. In 1938, the same year his wife was made an *Ehrenarier* (honorary Aryan), the following remarkable incident occurred. Someone had photographed the celebrated composer in a compromising position with another woman. The blackmailers wanted money, but when they turned up for a second time Lehár asked SS *Sturmbannführer* Hans Hinkel, his protector at the Reich's Ministry of Propaganda and Entertainment, to resolve the matter and keep it out of the public eye.

In the letter Lehár wrote to Hinkel, which has been preserved, Lehár follows his "Heil Hitler" with complaints about "Jewish blackmailers" and a "notorious Jewish lawyer." The epistle ends with the following: "You will have drawn the same conclusion, that a once esteemed artist is being treated like an outlaw by Jewish lawyers and the like." The blackmailer was thrown into prison — as was the lawyer, Max Eitelberg who, after his sentence, was deported and murdered in Kaunas, in Lithuania. In 1945 Hinkel sent Lehár a "Heil Hitler" with festive good wishes for the New Year.

After the war Lehár refrained from making any statement about his wartime behavior. He would only say that politics is sordid, and he did not wish to talk about vile things. And how could it be his fault that Hitler loved his *Merry Widow*?

Three great composers later offered musical commentary on that strange love story. In his *Leningrad Symphony*, Dmitri Shostakovich alluded to "Da geh' ich zu Maxim" from *The Merry Widow* to symbolize the German invasion. Béla Bartók did something similar in his *Concerto for Orchestra*. In the "Intermezzo interrotto" movement (*nomen est omen*), he parodies Shostakovich's earlier parody. Then Bartók lets everything descend into an infernal din of marching boots, which trample on the poet's works. But perhaps Dmitri Tiomkin trumped them both. In the film score he wrote for Alfred Hitchcock's *Shadow of a Doubt*, he used the waltz from *The Merry Widow* as a leitmotif for Uncle Charlie, the deranged mass murderer. A marriage made in heaven.

Herbert Ritter von Karajan
A Member of the Party

Herbert Ritter von Karajan is perhaps the best remembered of all the musicians who, during the war, had
some connection with Nazism, either as victims, opponents, or collaborators. His career didn't reach its peak
until after the war. Yet, even following his death in 1989,
he is still seen as an iconic conductor, commanding
admiration from everyone. Well, not quite everyone; he's
also been subjected to considerable pushback because of
his apparent links with the fascist regime. So just how
tainted was this man, who not only glittered on the concert stage but displayed equal flamboyance in his home
movies, on his luxury yacht, or in the cockpit of his private jet?

Von Karajan, a born Salzburger, was in his late twenties when Nazism emerged. In 1929 he had completed
his musical education in Salzburg and Vienna. That
same year he began his conducting career at the Stadt-
theater (civic theater) in Ulm, Germany. Then, between
1934 and 1942, he conducted concerts and operas in

the city of Aachen, a once important musical metropolis, An appointment soon followed with the Berliner Staatskapelle (Berlin State Opera). After the war, it was as if nothing had happened. He received one significant and lucrative engagement after the other: with the London Philharmonic and other major London orchestras, with the Berlin Philharmonic and the Vienna State Opera. Von Karajan was seen as a supreme being, and he behaved accordingly.

There is a fitting anecdote centering on von Karajan: three legendary conductors are having coffee and trying to work out which is the greatest of all time. Karl Böhm says that he is undoubtedly the best, his argument being, "The audience proves it at every concert!" A frown crosses Leonard Bernstein's magnificent brow, and he claims the honor for himself: "I am the greatest conductor because God told me so himself!" Von Karajan thinks it over and says, "Hmm, I don't remember saying that." That joke speaks volumes about von Karajan's godlike status within the world of music. He was the chief conductor of the greatest orchestras and the boss of the most prestigious summer event, the Salzburg Festival. He had a lot of clout with the most influential record company, Deutsche Grammophon Gesellschaft, and he also held sway in music management circles. He had a tremendous amount of power and could make or break careers, something he often did. In fact, he was a sort of führer himself, especially when standing in front of an orchestra. It's no wonder that authoritarian leaders admired him. Margaret Thatcher, for instance, was jealous of his perfect power. Von Karajan was the one who, in Salzburg, is reported to have uttered the famous words: "I am a dictator!" Funnily enough, Hitler wasn't crazy about him; he didn't care for his style. The Führer found von Karajan's habit of conducting from memory, without a score, particularly arrogant. Hitler's favorite conductor was Wilhelm Furtwängler. So how did von Karajan manage to hold his own during the Nazi era and garner international fame after the war? Let's start with the postwar period.

The von Karajan Wonder

In 1946 von Karajan met Walter Legge in Vienna. Legge, a London-based EMI record boss, had just founded the Philharmonia Orchestra. He hoped that orchestra would work primarily in the studio, producing records. To this end, he was on the hunt for a competent and charismatic chief conductor, one with enormous personality and box office appeal. Legge was a shrewd businessman first and a music lover second. Von Karajan had recently turned up in Vienna after lying low in Italy for a while after the war. Legge watched him at work during a rehearsal in Vienna and knew right away: He's my man! But a few hours before that concert was to take place, von Karajan had been forbidden to conduct in public. The celebrated conductor later wrote that the ban had been issued for "inexplicable reasons." At best, an astonishing remark: denazification was in full swing, and von Karajan had without a doubt been one of the standard-bearers of the Hitler mindset. One critic even called him *Das Wunder Karajan.* So it's no surprise that the authorities wanted to look into his wartime activities. But as the saying goes, problems are there to be solved. The canny Legge saw an opportunity: if von Karajan was prohibited from conducting in public, it didn't mean he wouldn't be allowed to make records.

Legge managed to talk around the high command in Great Britain, and he took his treasure back with him to London. There, in the celebrated Abbey Road Studios, von Karajan and the Philharmonia Orchestra made some 150 recordings. An international star was born, thanks to developments in the modern record turntable, then the LP, the discovery of stereo, and last but not least, a sophisticated advertising strategy. Legge and von Karajan created a revolution in music history: from then on, records—and not the concert hall—would determine a musician's success. Later, when CDs were launched, von Karajan would again take the lead.

As a result, he has one of the largest discographies in the world. Nevertheless, he showed little gratitude toward Walter Legge. When Legge was fired in 1963, von Karajan did nothing to help the man who launched his international career, even though he could easily have found him a suitable position.

But going back to those turbulent war years: What accusations can be brought against the maestro? On 7 April 1933, every Jewish civic employee was abruptly fired without compensation. Within a musical context, this included the staff and musicians of opera houses, orchestras, broadcasting orchestras, music schools, and music conservatories. In November of that same year, Joseph Goebbels took matters further by declaring that everybody who wished to work in the cultural sector had to become a member of the Reichskulturkammer, the Reich Chamber of Culture.

The SS officer Hans Hinkel was in charge. He carefully checked every candidate's details for racial purity and political affiliation. No one who was Jewish or left-wing was admitted. The rest — virtually everyone else — were allowed to work, and many were exempted from military service. This left musicians with two choices: either join the Reich Chamber of Culture or leave the country. Many of the biggest names emigrated, with a few exceptions such as Richard Strauss and Hans Pfitzner (though neither joined the Nazi Party).

Joining wasn't even a prerequisite for Hitler; he viewed artists as politically irrelevant and naïve. He didn't care, as long as they were discrete about their opposition to the new order. But Herbert von Karajan sprang into action, joining the Nazi Party the day after the new law was announced on 7 April. At the time, he had been visiting his parents in Salzburg. When von Karajan returned to Ulm, where he was then working, he joined the Nazi Party again, because it had been outlawed in Austria. It goes without saying that he also joined the Reich Chamber of Culture, although at first, this didn't offer him any benefits. Ulm had decided to sack him.

A brief but challenging period followed. Eventually, he was offered the position of Generalmusikdirektor in Aachen, a position with a political aftertaste. In Aachen, the managing director was Edgar Gross, a notorious SS officer. He sidelined a less flamboyant Nazi, Peter Raabe, in favor of von Karajan. In consolation, Peter Raabe was then asked to succeed Richard Strauss as the head of the Reich Chamber of Music. Von Karajan never denied his Nazi Party membership, although he claimed not to have signed up in Salzburg. He said he became a member in Aachen when he signed his contract there. According to von Karajan, a civil servant had shoved a stack of documents in front of him. One was for membership in the Nazi Party. And yes, he had signed because he wanted that job so desperately. He once said that he would have killed for that position because, at the time, he didn't have enough to eat. So why shouldn't he have signed?

Later on, however, he tried to pass himself off as a *Muss* Nazi, meaning someone who joined the Nazi Party under duress. However, his eager and undeniably spontaneous joining of the Nazi Party in Salzburg refutes that claim.

K

In Aachen, von Karajan was the youngest general music director in the entire country. He was just twenty-seven: blond, young, and dynamic. His conducting style was elegant, and he was a stickler for perfection. He was precisely the powerful archetype the regime needed as a cultural symbol. He had started working his way to the top, and the timing was perfect: Jewish conducting stars like Otto Klemperer and Bruno Walter had left Germany. Their departure, along with that of other leading musicians, created a gaping hole in the world of German and Austrian music. A talented newcomer like von Karajan was more than welcome. He not only ruled the musical life in the city of Aachen: he was also invited to guest conduct in many other important cities, including Brussels and Amsterdam. When, in 1938, he was allowed to conduct the Berlin Philharmonic, he became a favorite of the Nazis. That same year, he created an uproar in Berlin at the State Opera: first with *Fidelio* by Beethoven and then with Wagner's *Tristan und Isolde*. Those performances earned him the headline, "The von Karajan Wonder." He also became the star of a tussle between himself and Wilhelm Furtwängler.

Furtwängler's dislike of von Karajan was such that he refused to speak the man's name. He referred to von Karajan simply as "K." Hermann Göring, who was in charge of the State Opera, and Goebbels, who was von Karajan's patron and protector, were happy to have von Karajan in their camp. They could pit him against Furtwängler, an older man who could be meddlesome. Göring asked Heinz Tietjen, who managed the theaters, to promote their young god as much and as fast as possible, so von Karajan was assigned all the plum projects.

These included being asked to grace Hitler's birthday and to conduct in commemoration of the Anschluss (the annexation of Austria). He also conducted a work by a lesser Nazi composer, Richard Trunk, whose composition concluded with an arrangement of the "Horst Wessel Song" (also known as "Raise the Flag"), with exuberant lyrics about "Jewish blood spattering our knives." Trunk had shamelessly set to music the texts of Baldur von Schirach, a Nazi politician and head of the Hitler Youth.

Von Karajan was also sent abroad to conduct as a cultural ambassador. He was the Nazis' glamorous front man, but he also had feet of clay, as proved by his disappointing 1939 performance of Wagner's *Meister-singer*. This embarrassing performance cost him points in Hitler's good books. And, behind von Karajan's back, the city council of Aachen had appointed another conductor, named Paul van Kempen, because von Karajan was away too often, fulfilling other obligations.

Gradually, von Karajan's bond with the regime started to fray. The Führer didn't care for him. In 1942 von Karajan married Anita Gütermann, from a textile manufacturing family. She was the second of his three wives. Her father ran a factory making thread for sewing machines. Anita Gütermann was part Jewish through her grandfather; what was called a *Vierteljüdin*. This also didn't help von Karajan's cause with Hitler, but it didn't exactly hurt his chances, either. Hitler knew that von Karajan could be a useful pawn. Goebbels personally halted the judicial inquiry into Anita's Jewish roots. There's a grim detail: Anita's father joined the Nazi Party in 1933, hoping to supply them with brown silk for SS uniforms. When his Jewish ancestry was discovered, he was forced to formally leave the party, although his company flourished for the rest of the war. The Gütermann family was left unscathed.

Back in Aachen the celebrated conductor lost his job, not because of his wife's background but because he was away so often that his position was no longer tenable. Von Karajan saw an appointment to the prestigious orchestra in Dresden slip through his fingers. He had also conducted a "questionable" work by Gottfried von Einem, which ended up on the forbidden list immediately after its premiere because it contained jazzy elements. The end of the war approached, and von Karajan continued conducting until the beginning of February 1945. One of his final concerts of the war era was in honor of the victims of the Allied bombing of Dresden.

Von Karajan was busy with a plan to avoid the threat of reprisals; he suspected that German defeat was imminent. He flew to Milan and cooled his heels in a friend's home on Lake Como. He became one of the last of the dubious conductors to be nabbed after the war. He was sent to Salzburg in a truck. "Like animals," according to the man who had never uttered a compassionate word about the thousands of Jewish people and others similarly transported to their deaths. After a brief respite in his parents' home, he was interrogated. The charges were substantial: membership in the *Sicherheitsdienst*, spying on fellow musicians, betraying Jewish and left-leaning colleagues, and working closely with the despicable regime. He had a lot to explain.

Von Karajan denied all the charges; he would only admit to having been a member of the Nazi Party. Moreover, he had signed up under duress and thought he should be forgiven in light of the turbulent times. His judges were split along American and Soviet lines:

suggestions ranged from an outright acquittal to a long-term or lifelong ban on ever performing in public again.

Nazi or Opportunist?

While these discussions were taking place, von Karajan received incredible offers, including one from the Salzburg Festival in his native city. He had rustled up an orchestra and had started rehearsing when the Americans called a halt: they wanted him to wait until the entire denazification process had been completed and a decision had been reached. Then, lo and behold! Walter Legge turned up. He didn't give a fig about von Karajan's war history. In fact, Legge would later marry Elisabeth Schwarzkopf, another former Nazi Party member. And even before von Karajan's ban on performing had been lifted, the Lucerne Festival appointed him artistic director for life.

All in all, his conducting hiatus lasted thirty months. His punishment was harsh when compared with similar cases. His stern appearance, haughty demeanor, and his refusal to admit to anything, express regret, or even show compassion for the victims certainly did not help. Starting from 1947, von Karajan was allowed to conduct again — although, in the United States, there were protests every time he showed up to lead a concert or an opera. The most damaging thing is that he based much of his freedom on the argument that he had resisted *das Reich!* How? By marrying a Jewish woman, and because he wasn't in Hitler's good books.

When his rival Furtwängler died in 1955, von Karajan was appointed chief conductor of the Berlin Philharmonic. He insisted on a lifetime appointment. Two years later, he added his position at the Vienna State Opera. Everywhere he went, von Karajan put his stamp on the entire operation and the artistic vision. As soprano Birgit Nilsson once said, he would not tolerate any opposition. The various explanations for that quote prove yet again how shaky a personal interpretation can be. Person A might say that it was because, during the Nazi era, von Karajan had suffered so much opposition, but person B just thinks that von Karajan was himself a dictator.

Although events have receded into the past, von Karajan's genuine wartime role continues to fascinate many music lovers and historians. The researchers almost unanimously agree that, although he was not an avid Nazi, he had undoubtedly used his connections with the new order to maximize his superstar status. Even Helmut Schmidt, the former West German chancellor, called von Karajan an opportunist. But he had immense drive, burning ambition, and enough unscrupulous cunning to land him in the same category as the bad guys. Until the day he died, von Karajan did everything he could to forget, deny, minimalize, and even erase his tracks. He once compared his joining the Nazi Party with joining an *Alpenverein* (mountaineering association), or becoming a member of a sports club. But his devotion to the Nazi Party went beyond simply realizing his artistic dreams.

Some impartial scientific sleuths have assembled material that presents a less than rosy picture. Their evidence may not always be watertight, but the clues are so numerous it seems von Karajan may not have been all that innocent. These researchers argue, for example, that he was quick off the mark to join the Nazi Party, even at a time when there was little pressure to do so. That's one way of looking at things. But there are also documents.

Klaus Riehle has found written evidence indicating that von Karajan played an active political role. He discovered a statement made by a British member of the Allied Denazification Department: von Karajan's name had turned up in a 1943 index, listed as an agent for the *Sicherheitsdienst*—from the SS's intelligence division—in Aachen, suggesting he may have spied on his colleagues. Von Karajan maintained he had never served in the Wehrmacht. However, Riehle also uncovered a list in the Berlin Admiral Palace listing wages paid to members of the Wehrmacht, and von Karajan's name is on it. Riehle cites a group of witnesses—including von Karajan's wife, Anita—who admitted seeing him in a Wehrmacht uniform. The soprano Elisabeth Schwarzkopf, also a member of the Nazi Party, once said rather cryptically in a radio interview: "This is a case that has always been misreported, and I don't really want to correct it, because it's so terrible and I can't make it public at all. If I were to tell the truth, people would wonder, and I do not want that, because he was such a great musician."

The Viennese historian Oliver Rathkolb dug into von Karajan's past and discovered that von Karajan had been a junior member of Pan-German Gymnasium Rugia in Salzburg. Rathkolb also found letters from that time containing anti-Semitic remarks, such as one von Karajan wrote to his parents referring to the *Judaized Volksoper*. He did not wish to conduct there because the whole of Palestine would be in the audience. In Rathkolb's opinion, those statements point to von Karajan's direct progression to Nazi Party membership. According to Rathkolb, von Karajan concocted a story to ensure his denazification, which — although not correct — he later started to believe himself.

Joseph Schmidt
The German Caruso

In 1935 when Joseph Schmidt belted out the title song from the Austrian film *Heut ist der schönste Tag in meinem Leben* (Today is the most beautiful day of my life), he may have had mixed feelings. Perhaps he was still holding out hope for a favorable shift in German policy. But by then he had likely seen enough to make him doubt one of the following verses: "Morgen ist's vielleicht vorbei" (It might all be over tomorrow).

As a ten-year-old boy, I heard that love song when I saw the 1958 film *Ein Lied geht um die Welt* (A song goes around the world) about the life of the "German Caruso." The song made me a fan of classical music in general and vocal music in particular. From that day on, Joseph Schmidt became, in my eyes, the greatest tenor of all time, and so he has remained. Until my dying breath, I will cherish the LP that I bought with the entire contents of my piggy bank, *Unvergessener Joseph Schmidt* (The unforgettable Joseph Schmidt).

My appreciation naturally stems from Schmidt's

unique vocal color and stunning intensity, but it is perhaps slightly influenced by his heart-wrenching story as well. I am in good company, because many consider him the greatest tenor who ever lived. He was enormously musical and a giant in real life, although he was small in stature, standing just four feet eleven inches tall. When he recorded the hit mentioned above, Schmidt was just thirty-one and at the peak of his fame, which had been growing gradually since the late 1920s. But of course, his success didn't happen by itself.

Joseph Schmidt was born in Davydivka, a small hamlet in the Bukovina region, somewhere in what was then the immense Austro-Hungarian Empire. Davydivka would later become part of Romania and is now in Ukraine. The region's ethnic groups were successively ruled by one sphere of power or the other; the area was also a melting pot for various groups, languages, cultures, and forms of musical expression. The Jewish Schmidts, despite their German-sounding name, were part of the Romanian language group. Joseph picked up Hebrew at home, and at school he learned German and, later, French. When the violence of the First World War came too close for comfort, Schmidt's father, Wolf, moved the family to Chernivtsi, a larger city with an international population. There, he hoped to earn enough money to support his family.

Joseph or "Jossale" joined the Schmidt family in 1904, the third child, born after his sisters, Regina and Betty, and before his brothers, Schlomo and Mariem. He undoubtedly picked up his love of music from his mother, who sang folk tunes and religious songs. Joseph's father was a rather introverted, deeply religious Jewish man who had little affinity for music. He dreamt of his son becoming a doctor or a lawyer, and for a long time he resisted his son's burgeoning singing career, but to no avail. Young Joseph sang at parties in the village and in the synagogue. The pocket money he earned was a welcome addition. Joseph liked to sneak out of the house to sit for hours at the edge of the forest, quietly listening to the music of the Roma people who had set up camp. In fact, he would continue to nurture his love of musical diversity throughout his career. He sang Jewish religious music and popular tunes like "A Star Falls from Heaven" with the same conviction as the dramatic aria "Glück, das mir verblieb" from Erich Korngold's *Tote Stadt*. A number like "A Star Falls from Heaven" might surprise some classical afficionados. But tenors— including Jonas Kaufmann, Enrico Caruso, Beniamino Gigli, Luciano Pavarotti, Plácido Domingo, Rolando Villazón, Juan Diego Flórez, the list is endless—are known for including popular songs in their repertoire.

The Eighth Wonder of the World

Joseph Schmidt's innate talent was bolstered by lessons in piano, violin, and singing. And thanks to his unique voice, he also began singing in the local synagogue, which in turn brought him into contact with the world of theater. When the local German-language opera or operetta company needed a children's choir, they often turned to the boys who sang in the synagogue. They were good singers and knew how to read. After his appearance on stage, Joseph would often hang around backstage to enjoy the rest of the performance and pick up some tips.

When his voice changed, Schmidt lost his high boy-soprano register. In its place, he developed a remarkable tenor. He continued to sing in various local choirs and at the synagogue until there was no denying that his future would lie in the world of music. Many thought he would be perfect for the job of cantor, but his appointment fell through because he was too short. (Apparently, a divine voice was not enough.) When Schmidt was twenty, he debuted in his home city with his first solo recital, which was enthusiastically received. But, of course, his voice still needed to be shaped, and for this he went to Berlin.

Schmidt's uncle Leo Engel, who later became his agent and assistant, arranged and paid for singing lessons with Hermann Weissenborn, who would later have Dietrich Fischer-Dieskau as a pupil. Schmidt's studies were interrupted by a two-year stint in the army, though even as a soldier he remained musically active — not as a singer but, rather, as a pianist, violinist, or even a drummer in jazz orchestras. When his service ended in 1927, he returned to Berlin. His concerts there were enormously popular, but it was the radio that truly launched his career. In the early 1920s, the medium had grown viral, helping determine who would become famous and who would not.

In 1928 Schmidt auditioned for the Berlin Radio Network. The head of the opera division was a Dutchman named Cornelis Bronsgeest, and he was incredulous when he saw the tenor's small stature: Schmidt's head was barely visible above the piano. Bronsgeest was even more taken aback when Schmidt announced he would sing the stretta from Giuseppe Verdi's *Il Trovatore*. Bronsgeest apparently remarked: "Why doesn't he sing *Parsifal* while he's at it?" referring to a demanding role requiring a full-bodied heroic tenor. But when Schmidt opened his mouth, Bronsgeest could not believe his ears. That was the start of Schmidt's brilliant career, which quickly spread beyond the German-speaking world. In January 1929 the Jewish community in Antwerp invited Schmidt to sing in the local synagogue; that was Schmidt's first foreign performance. It was only after his radio debut in Berlin with the aria "O paradis sorti de l'onde" from Giacomo Meyerbeer's *L'Africaine*, along with a stunning *Idomeneo*, that he became a true international star.

A stream of successful films followed, all featuring Schmidt's singing voice. There were live performances in the Großes Schauspielhaus in Berlin, the Musikverein in Vienna, and celebrated venues in Switzerland, Salzburg, Mexico, Cuba. He even sang in Carnegie Hall in New York. International radio stations were also happy to have Schmidt as a guest, including the Dutch VARA and radio stations in Belgium. For Belgian audiences, he sang in the hall of the Antwerp zoo, known today as the Elisabeth Hall. In 1936 in Amersfoort, the Netherlands, he gave an outdoor concert during a summer festival attended by ten thousand people, although some claim the number exceeded one hundred thousand. Joseph Schmidt's concerts were notorious for their traffic jams, counterfeit tickets, and rabid journalists, as well as the ecstatic reactions from fans. Once when he happened to attend a concert at the Vienna State Opera, the audience gave him a prolonged ovation.

In 1933 he moved to the Grand Hotel in Vienna; he was famous in that Austrian city, and the Jewish issue in Berlin had started to turn ugly. As of 1 April that year, all of Schmidt's radio appearances had been canceled because the broadcasting network had been *gesäubert* — cleansed — of Jewish influences. He continued to sing in Berlin's concert halls, for an exclusively Jewish audience, until the autumn of 1936. His work in films also dried up — even though, at the premiere of *Ein Lied geht um die Welt* in May 1933, the ovation was earthshaking, including bravos from Joseph Goebbels. That song really did go around the world. In 1937 in the United States

Schmidt's fame was so great that there was talk of two world wonders: the Golden Gate Bridge in San Francisco and Joseph Schmidt! With so much international acclaim still ringing in his ears, he returned to Berlin in 1937, where everyone urged him to leave as quickly as he could. But maybe he would be able to stay put? Hadn't Goebbels himself recently applauded him?

Goebbels and Hitler regarded non-Aryans — including Jewish and Romani people, Blacks, homosexuals, and Slavs — as *Untermenschen*. Nevertheless, the Führer and his cohorts were sometimes remarkably impressed by the talent of such a "specimen." Because they could not admit as much in front of their supporters, they came up with a solution based on Goebbels's motto, *Wer Jude ist bestimme ich* (I decide who's Jewish). Goebbels introduced the title of *Ehrenarier* or honorary Aryan, with which the Nazis could save their own reputations and the fate of their favorite artists or scientists. If Joseph Schmidt had accepted that title, it would have meant "safe conduct" for his music and the undying admiration of the "great leaders." In fact, "Heut ist der schönste Tag" might have made a suitable anthem for the regime. It had an optimistic message set to a lively march rhythm. However, individuals were free to refuse the honorary title of *Ehrenarier*, and that is precisely what Joseph Schmidt did — with all the implied consequences. Following his tours in America and Europe, he felt it was time to search for new pastures. So with his partner, Lotte, and their son, Otto, Schmidt left Vienna. It was 7 March 1938, just in the nick of time, five days before the Anschluss, the German annexation of Austria. Destination: unknown.

The Great Singer's Odyssey

Schmidt's next port of call was Brussels, which briefly became his safe haven, where he could rest after his international tours. On 15 December 1938, he was the guest of honor at the annual gala for the foreign press. The German government threatened to expel all German journalists and embassy staff from the room if Herr Schmidt sang even a single word in German. The organizers limited the singer to songs in French, Italian, and Romanian. The following year, in the Brussels Royal Theatre of La Monnaie, one of Schmidt's dreams became a reality: he sang the role of Rodolfo in twenty performances of Giacomo Puccini's *La Bohème*, with additional performances in other major Belgian cities. It was Schmidt's first appearance in a genuine opera. He had missed out on many roles because of his small stature, although that was less of an issue in movies, where technical tricks could be put to use. However, audiences in Brussels did not view his size as a handicap. When the Germans occupied Belgium in 1940, Schmidt stayed in the capital, and he would have liked to remain. In September, he gave a concert in the Brussels Center for Fine Arts, attended by German military personnel. The Royal Theatre of La Monnaie also offered him a new leading role: Eleazar in *La Juive* by Jacques Halévy, although the project never saw the light of day. In the meantime, in Germany, a distasteful article about Schmidt was making the rounds. Beneath his photograph were the words: "Shown here is the former German radio singer, Joseph Schmitt [*sic*]. A criminal type whose picture belongs on every arrest warrant."

When the situation in Brussels became too hot to handle and the Gestapo were after him, Schmidt decided to leave. He was not granted a visa for the United States, so his friends took him across the French border. This was the beginning of a genuine odyssey. Schmidt went via Paris to Marseille, where thousands of applicants for asylum waited like penned cattle for a visa and travel documents. The German writer Anna Seghers has written a gripping novel about the uncertainty and frenzied mood of those times, called *Transit*. But again, Schmidt was plagued by bad luck. He waited, commuting between Marseille and Nice, giving hastily planned concerts in Grenoble or Avignon. His performance at the opera on 14 May 1942 in Avignon was his last public appearance.

All his waiting turned out to be in vain; he could have been a character from the novel *Transit*. Refugees had to have the correct certified documents. But when Schmidt had finally assembled the papers he needed to sail to the United States, it turned out someone else had taken his place on the ship. The mayor of Avignon offered to allow him to remain in that city (at the time, the south of France was still free), but the German threat was growing day by day. Local fascists were becoming more brazen, and by 11 November 1942, all of France was occupied. Yet, once again Schmidt managed to escape in the nick of time.

He set off on foot for Lyon, hoping to reach the Swiss border, the only option still available to him. His first attempt to cross into Switzerland failed; he had hidden in the woods with two women the whole night. When they finally reached the border in the morning, the border patrol sent them back to France. How history repeats itself! But on 8 October, they succeeded; the celebrated tenor was smuggled into the country on a hay wagon. He stayed in Zürich at Pension Karmel, which he knew from better times, but instead of recovering his strength, he became ill. The owner sent for a doctor. Before long, the entire world knew that the famous Joseph Schmidt was staying in Switzerland. However, he was not granted permission to go to the hospital; the Girenbad refugee camp was his next destination. "Hospitable" Switzerland had just passed a law exempting Jewish people from political refugee status. Therefore, the stateless Joseph Schmidt was sent to the Girenbad refugee center until his case had been investigated.

Joseph Schmidt was not killed by the Nazis. He managed to avoid the gas chambers. He wasn't hung on a meat hook or strangled. The Nazis didn't starve him or send him into a self-dug mass grave. But what happened to him in Girenbad was no less atrocious. Less than twenty miles from Zürich, Girenbad was no four-star hotel. "Guests" were housed in a former textile factory and forced to sleep on straw, guarded by soldiers. They were only permitted to leave the camp sporadically; one favorite destination was the nearby restaurant, Waldegg. There, displaced persons could rest and regain their sense of humanity. Joseph Schmidt would sometimes entertain his fellow guests with impromptu concerts, but the telltale signs of illness soon appeared: first laryngitis, then a bronchial infection. He was admitted to a hospital in Zürich but was treated there like a second-class citizen. When Schmidt complained of sharp pains in his chest, the doctors refused to examine him, suspecting him of creating a ruse to escape. He was discharged from the hospital on 14 November 1942. Two days later, back in Girenbad, he collapsed with pains in the region of his heart. The camp doctors didn't pay him any attention, but some concerned people carried him back to Waldegg. The landlady there was shocked when she saw his poor condition, and she let him rest on her couch. When she checked on him sometime later, he had stopped breathing. The most beautiful voice in the world had been silenced forever. The day after his death, the work permit he had applied for arrived. He would have been a free man. On his gravestone in the Unterer Friedhof Friesenberg in Zürich, flanked by two yew trees, are written the words, *Ein Stern Fällt!* (A star has fallen). Even in Switzerland.

In 2008, the astronomer Freimut Börngen named a small star after Joseph Schmidt — undoubtedly a touching gesture. But Schmidt's death remains, as the 1942 headline in the Basler Arbeiterzeitung said, *"Eine Schande für die Schweiz!"* (An embarrassment for Switzerland).

From Myra Hess to Vera Lynn
The Power of Music

During the First World War radio communication had been limited to military circles. But in the years before the Second World War, radio became a mass medium. This made a tremendous difference during the conflict; almost every citizen could gain information in an open and aboveboard way. Political leaders quickly recognized the importance of this new medium and tried to gain control of it. The accent, of course, was on military information, propaganda, and announcements. In Germany, the regime had control over radio broadcasts, and they hoped to achieve something similar in occupied territories. Belgium had its official NIR-INR network (the precursor of VRT-RTBF), and more than sixteen other, private stations. The occupying forces wanted to gain control of them all, and they succeeded to a large extent because many broadcasters did everything they could to remain on the air. The Germans wanted citizens to listen exclusively to their broadcasts, so Belgians were ordered to hand over their radios to keep them from listening

to the BBC. In exchange, they were given radios that could be tuned only to Brussel-Radio Bruxelles, a station under German control. All over the European continent, the BBC was the most important external network, not only for Belgium but also for the French. The BBC's Radio Londres, as it was called, denounced Radio Paris for collaborating with the Nazis. A French comedian named Pierre Dac was an announcer for the BBC during the war, and he used new lyrics to the well-known song "La Cucaracha" to point out to his countrymen: "Radio Paris, Radio Paris, Radio Paris is in German hands!"

This brings us seamlessly to music, which was very important during the war. During periods of conflict, church attendance grows, and music often assumes a healing, comforting, or uplifting role. The Second World War was no different. Music, like religion, provided a sanctuary for many civilians. It provided courage and strength to endure suffering, mourn human and other losses, keep up the fight against the enemy, and maybe relax and have fun. Most important, both popular and classical music helped people continue dreaming and hoping for a peaceful future. In Germany people listened to marches. In England a daytime program called "Music While You Work" was intended to calm British people contributing to the war effort. Classical music was used to keep up appearances, as if nothing was out of the ordinary. But there was also live music.

When the war broke out, the British government closed all the museums, music halls, theaters, and concert halls to prevent massive casualties in the event of a bombing raid. This may have been wise, but it left people with no cultural outlet. The pianist Myra Hess, an internationally renowned Londoner with a Jewish background, recognized a missed opportunity. She suggested to Sir Kenneth Clark, then director of the National Gallery, that he organize classical concerts in the empty museum, located in the heart of London in Trafalgar Square.

To the enemy, concerts there could hardly have been more symbolic or provocative. By then, the museum had been stripped of its artworks. All the paintings and sculptures had been carted away for safekeeping. To replace the artworks, the wartime government gave Clark permission to turn the museum into a temporary concert hall. For more than six years, lunchtime concerts were held every workday. People lined up around the block, hoping to be admitted. Hess performed, along with many of her famous associates, plus a legion of lesser gods and musicians from numerous military bands. The list of great names included the composer/pianist Francis Poulenc, the singer Pierre Bernac, and the violinist Jacques Thibaud. Lunch concerts cost one shilling, and according to the National Gallery 750,000 listeners attended, although other sources put the number above

840,000. Concerts were even held during the Blitz. The show always went on. One day, a bomb fell on one of the halls of the National Gallery, albeit not where the concerts were held. By the following day, the damage had been swept up, and it was back to business as usual.

Hess performed the first concert herself. She had invited some forty or fifty friends, expecting them to turn up out of pity, but more than one thousand interested listeners were there. They were hungrier for culture than for food, according to Clark. During that first concert, Hess played Scarlatti, Beethoven, Bach, Brahms, Chopin, and Schubert for an audience made up of listeners from all walks of life. There was quite an uproar when the concerts were suspended after the war. Many hoped they would continue, but this was not to be. The legendary Royal Albert Hall was another popular location for concerts, boxing matches, and political rallies. When the Queen's Hall was bombed, the popular Proms (Promenade Concerts) were moved there, and they have remained at the Royal Albert Hall to this day. But in all the concert halls, concerts could only be given during the day, and for a limited number of audience members.

The Hymn of Nations

Arturo Toscanini was one of the benefactors of Hess's lunchtime concerts. He also found other ways of keeping the population on their toes and prepared to fight the good fight. To him, national anthems were a perfect medium. They roused patriotic feelings and fueled intransigence and hostility toward the aggressor. Toscanini, the chief conductor of the American NBC Symphony Orchestra, used Giuseppe Verdi's choral work "Inno delle Nazioni" (Hymn of nations) to rouse popular sentiment. That one-movement cantata is an affecting, nationalist work for tenor and choir, composed in 1862, the period when new nations were being born, including a unified Italy. Verdi's original composition incorporates references to "God Save the King," the "Marseillaise," and "Il canto degli Italiani." Toscanini had performed the work in 1915 when Italy entered the First World War. He reprised the piece in the studio during one of his weekly live broadcasts with the NBC Orchestra, following Verdi's original score with his own arrangements of "The Star-Spangled Banner" and the Soviet "Internationale." Those additions symbolized the cooperation between the United States and the Soviet Union, two major powers, united in the fight against Hitler. By linking the anthems of those countries with Verdi, Toscanini created a musical alliance. What's more, doing so gave Mussolini and his followers a passing sneer. They had opted for a different national anthem — namely, "Giovinezza." In 1944 Toscanini's music was used as the soundtrack for a propaganda film.

However, when Igor Stravinsky tried to make a similar contribution, reaction was cool. In 1941 he had hoped to express his gratitude for being granted American citizenship by creating a new version — Stravinsky-style — of "The Star-Spangled Banner." It didn't go down well. The Boston police barred the performance during a concert conducted by Stravinsky himself. It seems that "tampering with the national anthem" was forbidden by law; dissonant versions were viewed as a slap in the face to the American people. It goes to show that it wasn't just the Soviet bosses and the Nazi leaders who opposed alien or anti-grassroots music.

Other national anthems played a supporting role in the war effort. Most were already in use, but during the war years, an extra dimension was added, more than just a new lick of paint. In 1922, for instance, Germany adopted the tune of the Austrian "Emperor's Hymn," written by Joseph Haydn and later used by Haydn in his string quartet, also known as the *Emperor Quartet*. It became the "Lied der Deutschen," with a verse containing the text *Deutschland, Deutschland über alles*, which has since been dropped. And no official Nazi ceremony was complete without the addition of the "Horst Wessel Song." While the French remained loyal to their "Marseillaise," the Vichy regime opted for "Maréchal, nous voilà!" in honor of collaborator Philippe Pétain. Until 1944 Russians sang the "Internationale," which was replaced by the current—wondrously beautiful—national anthem selected through a competition.

The Soviets were well acquainted with the impact of music on the morale of USSR citizens. Few large-scale classical works have been created under more tumultuous circumstances than Dmitri Shostakovich's Seventh Symphony. The symphony was aptly subtitled "Leningrad." The composer finished the score in December 1941 in Samara. It was initially dedicated to Lenin, but Shostakovich later amended the dedication in favor of the besieged city of Leningrad. The first performances took place on 5 March 1942 in Kuybyshev (as Samara was then known), a safe haven for numerous scientists and artists trying to escape the upheavals of war. Shostakovich's associates helped to organize the first performance of that symphony outside the country. Shostakovich had microfilmed the entire score, which was then smuggled through Iran, Egypt, and South America to the United States.

Arturo Toscanini and his NBC Symphony Orchestra played the American premiere of the piece in July 1942, making headline news. The symphony's composer appeared on the cover of *Time Magazine* dressed in a fireman's uniform; the portrait had not been retouched. It turns out Shostakovich had intended to join the army, but his poor eyesight and fragile physical condition meant he was assigned to a local unit at the conservatory.

He later joined the fire brigade. The most memorable performance of his *Leningrad Symphony* took place in Leningrad in August of that same year. The German army had surrounded Leningrad. Fear, deprivation, and famine devastated not only the civilian population but professional musicians as well. The Leningrad orchestra had been decimated: many players were either sick or dead. Yet the Soviet government did everything they could to ensure the concert took place. Army leaders sent any soldiers who were reasonably proficient on an orchestral instrument to fill in the vacant positions. When the conductor, Karl Eliasberg, discovered he was still missing a percussionist, he was told that the man, Dzaudhat Aydarov, had died. Eliasberg wanted proof, so he went to the morgue and found the man he was looking for on a pallet. Dzaudhat Aydarov, however, was still alive, if only barely; he was visibly moving and breathing. The percussionist was quickly patched up and took part in the concert.

To heighten the poignancy of the performance, the Soviets placed empty chairs among the musicians to symbolize those who were missing or dead. The concert was amplified with enormous loudspeakers so the entire civilian population could hear the piece and feel fortified by it. The music must have been audible to German troops, as well, banishing any hope that Leningrad was on the point of capitulating. The symphony referred directly to the circumstances of war: there are sounds of marching troops, military brass and percussion, a funeral dirge, apocalyptic moments, and in the end, the sound of opposition and victory. Long after the siege, Shostakovich's Seventh Symphony is still viewed as a musical symbol of rebellion and survival.

Classical Recipes

The music of earlier classical composers was regularly put to use during the Second World War. The German regime claimed Ludwig van Beethoven, but the English BBC used the first four notes of his Fifth Symphony as the theme for their news program, broadcast on Radio London. The message was double-edged: "fate" (the nickname of the Fifth) had struck, but those Germans shouldn't think they could adopt Beethoven's universal message — *alle Menschen werden Bruder* (all people become brothers, as he later explicitly stated in his Ninth Symphony) — for themselves. To use today's jargon, Beethoven is one of us. Because, hadn't that German with Flemish roots stood up to another dictator — Napoleon — in his day?

To hammer home its message, the BBC followed Beethoven's fate theme with a fragment from Handel's *Water Music*, another low blow. An eighteenth-century German composer, Handel was problematic for the Nazis, not because he was Jewish or Roma, but because he had left Germany for the land of the archenemy, England. He even went so far as to become an Englishman, something the British couldn't help boasting about. The Nazis also struggled with references to Judaism in Handel's work. They had to Aryanize his oratorio *Judas Maccabaeus* before it could be performed. The British liked to use Handel's music to thumb their noses at Germany. Art and indeed music know no boundaries. Bach was claimed by both sides as "one of our own." Germany had problems with the composer because his cantatas and passions often mentioned Judaism. The Nazis revised the *St. Matthew Passion*, omitting sentences like *von den Kindern Israels* (from the children of Israel) and *Dies ist Jesus, der Judenkönig* (He is Jesus, the king of the Jews), and there are recordings to prove as much. On the other side of the channel Great Britain was not lacking in its own odd, shortsighted reactions. The British musical hero Ralph Vaughan Williams protested vehemently when, during a service in London's Saint Paul's Cathedral to honor D-Day, Bach's "Ein feste Burg ist unser Gott" (A mighty fortress is our God) was performed. He thought German music had no place in D-Day celebrations, but perhaps the work's message had escaped him. It was all very confusing: some German composers were boycotted because their copyright fees went to a hostile nation. This held true for the Italians Giuseppe Verdi and Giacomo

Puccini and the Finn Jean Sibelius. Italy was of course an ally of Hitler's, and Finland, with its Continuation War against the Soviet Union, was also firmly in the enemy camp. Figuring out which composers were suitable for broadcast was a delicate balancing act in many countries.

The Germans also used heavy artillery of a musical sort, including a piece by Franz Liszt, even though he was actually an ethnic Hungarian. The Nazis used a fanfare from Liszt's *Les Préludes* before announcing their military victories in Russia — or their lack thereof. They added military drums to the fragment, calling it the "Russian Fanfare." Even after Stalingrad, when there were no more German victories, Nazi belligerence continued. They drew upon the text accompanying Liszt's symphonic poem, something Liszt had regularly done to help listeners understand what they were about to hear. Liszt used the word *Sturmsignal* (the trumpet sounds the alarm) to refer to war and battle. For Liszt, however, it wasn't an actual war but the struggle of the ordinary individual who, in life, has to face not only pleasantries but hardship. Liszt, who died in 1886, should absolutely not be thought of as a follower of Nazism before the fact, even though he did become Richard Wagner's father-in-law. No trace of anti-Semitic symbols or statements can be attributed to him. On the contrary, he once formally declared: "I am no anti-Semite; I respect every decent person."

It's well known that, to the Nazis, Richard Wagner was beyond compare. His operas were primarily inspired by great Germanic history and sagas; moreover, he had made anti-Semitic statements in his book *Das Judenthum in der Musik* (Jewishness in music). He lashed out at Jews in general and Jewish musicians in particular, especially Felix Mendelssohn and Giacomo Meyerbeer. He accused them of superficiality and said they could not create genuine art. No wonder the German government banned their music.

But the Nazis took matters to the extreme. Even the music of Max Bruch ended up on their list. The composer of the famous violin concerto also wrote the popular *Kol Nidrei* for cello and orchestra, based on two Hebrew melodies. This landed him in the "Jewish" category, and his entire body of works was banned. But Bruch was a steadfast Protestant, as German as they come. Like many German citizens, he viewed the Jewish population as an integral part of German culture. Bruch wrote his oratorio *Moses* in his desire to continue the tradition of great vocal works based on biblical figures. In this, he was the artistic opposite of game-changer Wagner. Wagner's military-tinted overture from *Die Meistersinger of Nuremberg* was a hit in wartime Germany. It was used in a Nazi propaganda film and played at the start of every gathering of the Nazi Party in Nuremberg.

Germany understood the ability of broadcast music

to manipulate listeners. Not to browbeat them but to win them over. So German-controlled Radio Paris broadcast a lot of classical music and other selections. With its household names, big stars, and lively concerts, the German-minded station hoped to win listeners' hearts and foster the impression that life wasn't so bad under German rule.

Brass Bands, Movies, and Marches

Brass bands can be festive. They are also useful during battle to bolster the fighting spirit on the field and patriotic morale on the home front. Eugene Aynsley Goossens was a composer and leading conductor from a Flemish musical family from Bruges. His family had moved to England in the 1880s. His brother Leon became a world-famous oboist; Edward Elgar, Ralph Vaughan Williams, and Benjamin Britten all dedicated compositions to him. Between 1903 and 1906 Eugene Aynsley Goossens went to Bruges to study music. Back in England during the First World War, he commissioned leading British composers to write marches to be performed at the beginning of every public concert. This was such a success that Goossens repeated the exercise during the Second World War. But by then he had become the chief conductor of the Cincinnati Symphony Orchestra, so the composers he asked were primarily American. The list is impressive. Among the eighteen were William Grant Still, Bernard Wagenaar, Walter Piston, Darius Milhaud, and Henry Cowell. The only two works that are still programmed today are Morton Gould's "Fanfare for Freedom" and the enormously popular "Fanfare for the Common Man" by Aaron Copland.

Classical composers were also asked to write music for propaganda films. One, the American composer Marc Blitzstein, was from the political left, as is clear from a number of his compositions. He wrote *The Cradle Will Rock* about corruption and greed in the city of Steeltown, and an off-Broadway adaptation of the *Three Penny Opera* and other works by Brecht and Weill. Marc Blitzstein was stationed with the US Eighth Army in London during the war. One of his assignments was to write music for wartime films. He also composed *Free Morning* and *The Airborne Symphony*, a massive symphonic oratorio. It was written for a large orchestra and male chorus. Unfortunately, due to a lack of manpower, it wasn't performed until after the war. The story goes that Blitzstein lost the score on his way back to the United States. Fortunately, he was able to rewrite it from memory, and after the war Leonard Bernstein conducted the first performance. Needless to say, because of Blitzstein's socialist sympathies, he was targeted by the House Un-American Activities Committee, Joseph McCarthy's hobbyhorse.

The genre of light or popular music also played a crucial wartime role. Several songs can even be considered de facto hymns, including "The White Cliffs of Dover," "When the Lights Go On Again," and "We'll Meet Again," sung by the British Vera Lynn. The now lesser known singer Deanna Durbin also had a massive hit in the Anglo-Saxon world with her "Beneath the Lights of Home." Such songs weren't explicitly about the war, but in their lyrics, people recognized their own fears and longings for peace and better times. In Europe, Lale Andersen recorded the sentimental soldier's song, "Lili Marleen," and Zarah Leander sang "Ich weiss, es wird einmal ein Wunder geschehen" (I know a miracle will happen one day).

Wartime hits did not necessarily need lyrics. During the war, the legendary bandleader Glenn Miller gave up a lucrative career to join the US Army Air Force, playing hundreds of shows for the armed forces. His spirited brand of swing was also popular in living rooms. One number, "Jeep Jockey Jump," was a tribute to American soldiers. Soldiers on the front needed a boost in morale, and back home, dancing did wonders for everyone's wartime mood.

Hanns Eisler
The Revolutionary

For Hanns Eisler from Leipzig, there was no spectacular escape and no concentration camp; he was apparently unscathed by the war, but this makes him no less relevant. His mother, Ida Fischer, was a butcher's daughter (the name Fischer didn't really match her father's profession). Hanns's father was Rudolf Eisler, an Austrian philosopher born to a Jewish family. In 1901, when Hanns was barely three, the family moved to Vienna. As a child he began experimenting with music on his own. When he was ten he bought a book about basic music theory and composed his first piece — by ear, because his father was short of funds and had sold the family piano. Those early attempts at composition have all been lost.

When he was fourteen Eisler joined an Austrian socialist youth group, which gave his compositions a decidedly political flavor. He was sixteen when the First World War broke out. At the time the family was under scrutiny because Hanns's brother Gerhart published an anti-war periodical. Hanns wrote an anti-war oratorio,

Gegen den Krieg, based on texts by Bertolt Brecht. Eisler survived the First World War, despite having been stationed at the front for a considerable time. There, he was punished on numerous occasions for ignoring commands, and he was wounded a few times.

After that ordeal was over he signed up to attend the Viennese academy of music, but his stay there was brief: he found the teaching methods superficial and bourgeois. Instead, he decided to take lessons from Arnold Schoenberg who, with his *Moderne Musik*, had made a radical break with the pompous character of romantic and late romantic classical music. In 1923 Eisler completed his studies as Schoenberg's favorite disciple, and he was awarded the artistic medal of the city of Vienna; Richard Strauss had been a member of the jury. An uncertain period followed as Eisler tried to figure out what he wanted to achieve as a musician. He worked at various unfulfilling jobs, including editing at Universal Edition, the music publishers.

In the course of his years with Schoenberg, a difference of opinion had arisen about the role of the composer. The teacher and pupil were diametrically opposed. According to Schoenberg, who subscribed to the principle of art for art's sake, a composer who took the wishes of his audience into account could not be called a genuine artist. On the other hand, Eisler thought it was paramount to keep the listeners in mind. Composers had to encourage them, advise them, instruct them, and if possible, keep them out of the grip of fascism.

Eisler was less interested in the purely aesthetic than in conveying the message. When he moved to Berlin in 1925, that sentiment became his artistic calling card. There, he found a welcome hotbed of experimentation and flirtations with political engagement in every form of creative expression. He took to Berlin like a fish to water. Political engagement ran in the family. Eisler's brother Gerhart had become a communist journalist. His sister Elfriede, who first joined the social democratic movement when she was a student, became a cofounder of the German Communist Party (KPD). Between 1924 and 1925 she was the president of the politburo. However, after a year in office, she was sidelined for being too left-wing and succeeded by Ernst Thälmann. By then she had changed her name, not on a whim, but as a matter of principle. She decided to go through life as Ruth (a name with Hebrew origins) Fischer (her mother's maiden name).

The Break with His Teacher

There was a second reason for Eisler's rift with Arnold Schoenberg, one closely related to the first. In Berlin, Eisler's musical language—against his mentor's wishes—became contaminated with the sounds of folk music, jazz, and cabaret. Such influences fit Eisler's philosophy well, but they clashed with Schoenberg's highbrow vision. Eisler wanted to reach the masses, but he couldn't make much headway with the elitist and inaccessible tonal language of the Second Viennese School. So he turned his back on that episode, saying simply that he found Schoenberg's modern music unpleasant. Later, he conceded that his words had been needlessly ungrateful and harsh; he could have shown more respect to the man who had taught him for free. It comes as no surprise that Eisler found in Richard Wagner a far greater enemy. But there were two sides to that coin: while Eisler detested Wagner, the anti-Semite, he continued to value him as a musician. When Eisler died, an open score of *Tristan and Isolde* was found beside his bed.

Eisler dedicated himself unconditionally—as a composer and to a lesser extent as a pianist and conductor—to the working classes and the anti-fascist movement. He focused on writing communist choral works, revolutionary cantatas, marches, film scores, and all manner of music for the stage. He had a strong connection with a phenomenon known as workers' choirs. This movement had begun in the late nineteenth century when singers with a social democratic bent began to feel alienated in existing bourgeois choral societies. These workers' choirs sang a broad repertoire from opera to folk songs. Gradually, with the rise of fascism, they adopted a more political stance. Heated discussions took place, for instance, about performing Beethoven's *Missa Solemnis*. Some saw it as a remarkable artistic achievement for amateurs, while others thought the work simply confirmed the corrupt and collaborating ecclesiastical powers. With hindsight, you might say that both parties were right, but as the political and social polarization intensified, the choral groups became even more radical.

Starting from the 1920s such choirs were committed to peace, protest demonstrations, emancipating the working class, developing a socialist society, and anti-fascism. Eisler wrote *Kampflieder* or battle hymns to meet that need. They were part of the agitprop (a contraction of artistic *agitation* and *propaganda*) to counter the advancing fascist regime. The songs were intended for proletarian listeners and their intellectual allies and were primarily dark, boisterous, and rousing marches. One good example is "Einheitsfrontlied" ("United Front Song"):

Und weil der Mensch ein Mensch ist,
   Drum braucht er was zum Essen,
bitte sehr, Es macht ihn kein Geschwätz nicht satt,
   Das schafft kein Essen her.
Drum links, zwei, drei! Drum links, zwei, drei,
   Wo dein Platz, Genosse, ist
Reih' dich ein in die Arbeiterfront,
   Weil du auch ein Arbeiter bist.

And because a person is a person,
    he'll need something to eat, please!
He gets tired of prattle for it does not give him food.
So left, two, three! So left, two, three!
    To where your place is, comrade.
Join up with the workers' United Front,
    for you are a worker too!

This song, written in 1934, brought all the strands together. The lyrical content: during the Weimar Republic, friction had grown between workers aligned with the SDP or Social Democratic Party, and the KPD or Communist Party. After Hitler assumed control of Germany, more and more people believed the two parties should join forces to fight fascism, and the "United Front Song" was an open plea. Artistically, it was written in a strict marchlike tempo, simple enough for everyone to join in. The message was the important thing. The lyricist was Bertolt Brecht, one of the first text writers with whom Eisler collaborated in Berlin. Their lifelong friendship led to a fruitful artistic alliance. Just think of the individual songs on which they collaborated — such as the "Solidaritätslied" ("Solidarity Song"), the "Ballade vom Wasserrad" ("Ballad of the Waterwheel"), and the "Lied von der belebenden Wirkung des Geldes" ("There's Nothing Quite like Money").

Eisler also wrote music for a number of Brecht's plays,

including *Die Mutter* (*The Mother*), *Die Massnahme* (*The Decision*), *Schwejk im Zweiten Weltkrieg* (*Šchweik in the Second World War*), and *Galilei* (*Life of Galileo*). The "Einheitsfrontlied" was made famous by a singer who opposed Hitler, Ernst Busch. He was justly called "the Caruso of the barricades." Later, the singer Gisela May also sang Eisler's songs. Eisler's simple and militant music shows he understood that this segment of his oeuvre did not belong in the concert halls but on another stage: in the streets, where he performed it with his choir and singers.

Yet Eisler resisted limiting himself to writing singalongs that conveyed his leftist message. He continued to write original melodies, harmonies, and rhythms that displayed an advanced level of complexity; they may not have been as impenetrable as Schoenberg's music, but they were far from simple. One example is his *Zeitungsausschnitte*, based on newspaper clippings, as the title suggests.

Eisler also dabbled in film music, writing the score to Slatan Düdow's legendary German feature film, *Kuhle Wampe*. Released in the United States as *Whither Germany?* this 1932 film depicts a family that has been evicted from their apartment. They have no choice but to move to a Berlin tent camp called Kuhle Wampe. In German, *Kuhle* means "pit," and in the Berlin dialect, *Wampe* means "stomach," so together the words represent an empty stomach. The film's subject matter—unemployment, poverty, and struggle—was from the pen of, yet again, Bertolt Brecht. The leading role was played by none other than Ernst Busch. Eisler also wrote the score for Joris Ivens's 1932 documentary, *Komsomol (Song of Heroes)*. In that film about heroic Soviet workers building a steel plant in Siberia, Eisler contrasted folk songs with modern classical music, typical of the two styles he constantly alternated.

With this type of work, Eisler stood out unambiguously as an enemy of the Nazi regime. Unambiguous, but nevertheless two-pronged: simple melodies were targeted against the regime, while the more challenging passages were "degenerate." On top of it all, he was also Jewish. He left Germany a month after the fire in the Reichstag in Berlin. This was the start of a worldwide journey, taking him to Vienna, Belgium, the Netherlands, the Czech Republic, London, Paris, and the United States, where he lived for many years. During his time in the United States, he continued composing music. He also organized a benefit concert tour to raise money for children in the protected Territory of the Saar Basin. Those who took part included Ernest Hemingway, the composer Aaron Copland, and the musicologist Charles Seeger, the father of politically active folksingers Peggy and Pete. Eisler gave a talk before each concert to explain the situation.

Eisler first visited the New World in 1933. He addressed

meetings in Chicago during that trip, taught, and composed music. He also showed a keen interest in the film industry and visited MGM studios. There, he met some actors and he later wrote about the experience in the magazine *Deutsche Zentral-Zeitung*: "I am not exaggerating when I say that film artists, not just employees but actors as well, screenwriters and directors, are taking a more left-wing stance despite some of them being very well paid. They are becoming left-wing because they are disgruntled about their work, if only because everything revolves around making a profit in the film business."

Eisler also referred to Charlie Chaplin, who had planned to film a black comedy about the Good Soldier Schwejk with Peter Lorre in the lead, although that film was never made. In 1937 Eisler took part in the Spanish Civil War, where he wrote songs for the International Brigades (made up of volunteers from the United States and Europe) and organized concerts. It is fair to say that Eisler was no salon communist, sitting it out safely while others were doing the dirty work back home. He never stopped using his talents to fight fascism.

The Deportation

When the war broke out Eisler returned to the United States. He gained access to the film world, composing music for an advertisement directed by no one less than

Joseph Losey. Its remarkable title was *Pete Roleum and His Cousins*, about the history and importance of petroleum, and Eisler, together with Oscar Levant, wrote the music. Eisler commuted between two artistic centers throughout the war, New York and Los Angeles. He began work on the *Hollywood Songbook* with texts by Bertolt Brecht, Hölderlin, Goethe, and Rimbaud. The central theme was separation from one's homeland, and the work provides evidence that Eisler held art songs or lieder in high regard.

He wrote material for Broadway, and such film scores for Hollywood as Fritz Lang's *Hangmen Also Die*, a propaganda film made during the war about the notorious Deputy Protector of Bohemia and Moravia, the Reichsprotektor Reinhard Heydrich. Eisler wrote the score for *None but the Lonely Heart*, starring Cary Grant. Joseph McCarthy's House Un-American Activities Committee (HUAC) viewed the film as communist propaganda, although Eisler's score was nominated for an Oscar. He also became involved with social problems in his adopted country; he wrote songs protesting racial discrimination, such as the "Ballade vom Nigger Jim." And of course, Eisler had his own brush with the HUAC's hearings. When he was summoned to appear before that committee in 1947, the war was already over. He and his wife and his brother Gerhart were ordered to appear.

In all probability the most crucial witness in his case

was his sister Elfriede, known as Ruth. Her story is worthy of its own book. Witnesses describe Ruth Fischer (the former Elfriede Eisler) as a loose cannon, both rude and fanatic. When Hitler assumed power in 1933 she left Germany and emigrated to the United States, traveling first through Spain and then Cuba, a well-trodden route. Once there she switched sides and became vehemently anti-communist. She became the editor of an anti-Soviet newsletter. Between 1942 and 1955, she was a member of the Pond, a secret society devoted to uncovering all manner of espionage, both confirmed and suspected. Ruth even accused her brother Gerhart of terrorism, of assassinating *Genossen* (comrades), of atomic espionage, and of being a member of the Comintern, the Soviet cell advocating worldwide communism.

When her other brother, Hanns Eisler, came up for questioning by the HUAC, the committee focused on one of Eisler's compositions, *Die Massnahme*, based on a play by Bertolt Brecht in which four agitators intent on stirring up unrest in China murder one of their comrades, or *Genosse*, because he strayed from the party line. In this work a Greek chorus approves of the assassination. Whether that chorus represents the party, the working class, or the secret service, the HUAC believed the assassination stemmed from Stalinist dictatorship. Eisler tried to save his skin by minimizing the revolutionary content of the piece, and he was relatively successful. Several internationally renowned artists and scholars, including Stravinsky, Einstein, Picasso, and his friends Charlie Chaplin, Leonard Bernstein, and Woody Guthrie, organized benefit concerts to raise money for his legal defense. Perhaps their support ensured that Eisler wasn't jailed, although he and his wife were forced to leave the country. On 26 March 1948, that "technical deportation" brought him to East Berlin via London, Prague, and Vienna. He died there on 6 September 1962. He didn't feel at home in that East German regime, either. He regularly got into discussions with the government, but the honorable composer spent ten years teaching at the conservatory that now bears his name. For their part, the DDR received from Eisler a wonderful national anthem based on the text "Auferstanden aus Ruinen" ("Risen from Ruins").

Eisler left a remarkable souvenir in Belgium. The *Kalifornische Ballade* (*California Ballad*), which he had begun in Berlin in 1932, was finished in 1934 in London. It was background music for a radio play, one of his "applied" compositions. The story was by Ernst Ottwalt, who died in 1943 in a Siberian gulag. It involves the Swiss Johann August Sutter. When Sutter emigrated to America, he bought up vast tracts of land and ranches. The unscrupulous Sutter enslaved Native Americans and was known as the "Emperor of California." His life changed dramatically when, in 1848, gold was discovered on his land. Although he had a legion of soldiers on his payroll — he called himself "the general" — he was overwhelmed by the gold rush. Try as he might, he was unable to gain control of the natural resources, which he believed to be his sole property. He was simply over-run by the stampede of prospectors. He could not win the endless stream of legal battles that followed; he lost everything and died in Washington, DC, in 1880, bitter and penniless. The world premiere of Eisler's *Kalifornische Ballade* took place in Belgium on 7 December 1934.

Paul Douliez
From Socialist to Nazi

The radio play for which Hanns Eisler wrote the music *Kalifornische Ballade* had been put on the boycott list in Germany, so the premiere had to be held elsewhere. Before the war, German artists were warmly welcomed in Belgium and the Netherlands, especially those who had run into trouble in their own country. They regularly performed in Belgium, both in concert halls and on the radio. Eisler's *Kalifornische Ballade* was first performed in a Brussels radio studio belonging to the National Institute for Radio Broadcasting (NIR). A fascinating tidbit of Belgian national and musical history is associated with this broadcast. Sadly, no recording of the world premiere, performed on 7 December with soloists and the salon orchestra of the NIR, has survived. At that time the network had just started testing a system for recording music onto shellac-based discs, but the technique had not been perfected. Luckily, a second performance of the work took place in April 1935. By then the network had finished its testing. The play was

broadcast in a Dutch version made by Gust De Muynck, a writer and the first Flemish director of the NIR. In April, the conductor was no one less than Eisler himself, who happened to be a good friend of De Muynck's. The network had also invited Eisler's "personal singer," the legendary Ernst Busch; his Dutch wasn't half bad. A recording of that performance was made on shellac, but the disk had become damaged over the years. In 2017 the recording was masterfully restored and included as a bonus track on a new release of the songs accompanying the radio play made by the Dutch Ebony Band for the Berlin Classics label. Interestingly, the very first performance had not been conducted by Hanns Eisler but by a young Flemish musician named Paul Douliez, who worked at the network as a pianist and conductor.

The Nazis expounded their ideology within the cultural landscape of Dutch-speaking Belgium, as they had in every country they occupied. To the Nazis, culture—and indeed the medium of radio—provided an essential tool for spreading information and propaganda. And, as in Germany, some Belgian artists collaborated with the occupying forces for a variety of reasons. Some saw an opportunity to enhance their personal success, others hoped to achieve Flemish emancipation, and others were simply too afraid to resist. Countless reports and dissertations have been written about this subject; many have been published, and others can be accessed in libraries and research centers. Yet, many years after the fact, the issue remains sensitive and is handled with utmost circumspection. Most of the Belgian musicians who, in one way or another, helped the Nazis realize their goals usually limited themselves to relatively harmless activities. However, when it came to collaboration, Paul Douliez undoubtedly went beyond the pale.

Born in 1905 in Hasselt in the Belgian province of Limburg, he was known as Paul, though his given name was Polydore. He is perhaps better known to the postwar generation as the father of one of Belgium's greatest actresses, Yvonne Douliez, whose stage name was Ivonne Lex. She was a daughter from Douliez's marriage to the celebrated Antwerp actress Hélène Van Herck. Paul's father, Hendricus, was a member of the military band of the Eleventh Line Regiment, stationed in Hasselt, Limburg's capital. The father of Belgian politician Willy Claes, who later became the secretary general of NATO, was also stationed there. No surprise, then, that Paul and his brother Jan—who followed the same political path as his brother—became musicians. Their mother taught her children the basics of music. Paul Douliez died in 1989 in Stuttgart, Germany, which may hint at the political path followed by that Flemish pianist, conductor, composer, and author.

Paul Douliez's U-turn

Douliez received his earliest musical training at the Organ and Singing School in Hasselt, Belgium, an institution with a solid Flemish Catholic character. It closed its doors in 1967. An important Flemish composer, Arthur Meulemans, had been the school's director. After Douliez completed his musical education at the Antwerp Conservatory, unbeknownst to his tyrannical father and with outside financial help, he became a professional musician. At twenty-six, he was hired as a pianist and conductor by the NIR.

The network's 1934 annual report is a veritable Who's Who of the Belgian music scene. The NIR's music director was Désiré Defauw, born in Ghent. When the Second World War broke out, Defauw left for the United States, becoming an internationally renowned conductor. He was even the music director of the Chicago Symphony Orchestra for a time. According to that annual report, "the concerts of the Symphonic Orchestra were conducted by Arthur Meulemans and Jean Kumps. The concerts of the Radio Orchestra were conducted by Franz André and Paul Gason, and the concerts of the Genre Orchestra by Karel Walpot and Paul Douliez."

One of Douliez's duties, in addition to conducting, was composing. These weren't grand opuses but radio themes to introduce programs such as daily gymnastics.

He also composed symphonic works such as *Heide*, based on poetic prose written by his friend Hilarion Thans. And he orchestrated works by Corelli, Chopin, and other classics that were suitable for the radio. Douliez also wrote music for radio plays such as *Reinaert de Vos* by Yvonne De Man. When Belgians of that era come across De Man, they automatically think of Hendrik, Yvonne's brother, a socialist leader known as the "Man with the Plan for Labor." Yvonne De Man was married to Gust De Muynck, who also held socialist beliefs.

At first one might think it perfectly natural for Douliez to conduct the music of a communist such as Eisler. His job involved conducting, his higher-ups were left-leaning or anti-fascists, and Douliez had to obey orders from on high. But plenty of evidence indicates that Douliez stood firmly to the left himself. For example, the records of the Archive and Museum of the Socialist Labor Movement (AMSAB) in Ghent refer to a battle hymn for De Man's Plan of Labor mentioned above. The song's composer is listed as Paul Douliez. It seems unlikely he would have been offered the assignment if he hadn't been sympathetic to the socialists and their ideals. In addition, with the help of a former colleague, Herman van de Vijver, from the VRT (a national public service network in Belgium), I found a recording of a left-wing fighting song used during the Spanish Civil War. It's called "Am Rio Jarama," and it is sung by the revolution's star vocalist Ernst Busch. Lyrics: David Martin and Ernst Busch. Music: Paul Douliez.

There's more. Douliez wrote music for the 1937 International Workers' Olympiad in Antwerp. This event was an athletic and political response to Berlin's notorious 1936 Olympic Games. The Antwerp Olympiad celebrated the triumph of socialism and anti-fascism and supported the freedom fighters opposing Franco in Spain. Although the NIR covered that sporting event, Douliez's commission to write a composition wasn't part of that deal. All told, there's every indication that Douliez was decidedly left-wing. Other Belgian composers such as Jef Van Hoof or Gaston Feremans would never have been asked to compose such a politically charged piece of music.

But then along came the Nazis, and events took a dramatic turn. After the Germans invaded Belgium on 10 May 1940, they didn't waste any time. Almost immediately, under orders from the *Propaganda Abteilung*, they seized control of the radio studios housed in the striking Flagey Building, the home of the NIR network. No small feat, because when the Belgian radio bosses got wind of the impending invasion, they adopted a scorched earth policy, sabotaging not only the recording equipment in the Flagey studios but the transmission towers as well. The Germans rechristened the NIR Zender Brussels (in Dutch) and Radio Bruxelles (in French), using the network primarily to broadcast information — or what could be called propaganda. Under German control the station broadcast news about the war; attacks against Jews, communists, and allies; German lessons; and interviews with Nazi sympathizers such as Staf De Clercq, August Borms, Cyriel Verschaeve, Jef Van de Wiele, and even Joseph Goebbels himself.

Many of the network's Belgian bigwigs and a portion of the news team were immediately replaced, but a great deal of the employees stayed on. Among them were both pro- and anti-German elements. Douliez remained at his post in the music department, where he behaved like a dyed-in-the-wool Nazi. He tried to elbow his way to the top of the new network but lost out to someone named Wies Moens. Douliez became a member of the Flemish branch of the Algemeine SS. After a call to arms from Goebbels, on 12 May 1943, he joined the military branch or Waffen-SS with the rank of SS-Kriegsberichter (SS War Reporter Company). He then left for the Eastern Front, intent on serving the new rulers. He was awarded an Iron Cross, but his "real" reward followed later.

Douliez continued working in Brussels, where he conducted the various radio orchestras in his SS uniform. The programming of the broadcasts was quickly adapted: no more Eisler, Weill, or others of a communist ilk, no vulgar upstarts, and absolutely no Jewish composers like Darius Milhaud. Airtime went instead to the great German masters and Flemish composers. The scheduled programming included Belgian artists like Armand Preudhomme, Jef Van Hoof, Yvonne Verbeeck, and Eugene Traey, a pianist who for many years was chairman of the jury of the Queen Elisabeth of Belgium Competition. There was also "Nonkel Bob" (Uncle Bob) Davidse who, after the war, enjoyed singing South African songs.

Douliez also did his bit for the Germans outside the radio station, regularly attacking Judaism and plutocracy in the *Vlaamsche Land* newspaper. He argued for a responsible policy toward music, with no room for *bamboulas*, a word referring to a primitive type of African drum and later used as a pejorative for Blacks, particularly jazz musicians. He wanted to ban all Bolsheviks and Jewish people from appearing in concert halls, theaters, and on his radio networks. "His" being the operative word, because Douliez had managed to climb still higher up the hierarchical ladder. When Wies Moens, the network's general director, stepped down on 1 January 1944 to protest the creation of a Flemish branch of the Hitler Youth, Douliez lost no time in taking over. Zender Brussels remained on the air until the liberation of Belgium in September of that year.

Douliez proclaimed his belief that Germany would win the war until the bitter end. But things didn't turn out quite as he expected. He slunk off to Germany, along with other members of the defeated Waffen-SS. They weren't entirely convinced they had lost, so during their retreat, they hastily set up a radio station called Kampf-sender Flandern und Wallonien, just over the German border, first in Herkenrath, then in Wipperfürth. Douliez was again put in charge of that network, although the interlude was, of course, brief.

Condemned to Death

In May 1945 when Douliez was forty years old, he was standing on the roof of the radio building in Berlin — in the Masurenallee, to be precise. As bullets whizzed past his head, he described for German, French, and English listeners the futile efforts to defend the city from the Allies. Douliez's hopes of a German victory had turned to dust. Along with his comrades he was captured after a dramatic pursuit by Soviet soldiers, and he spent a long time in prisoner of war camps in Kyrgyzstan, Uzbekistan, Russia, and Romania. He later wrote a fascinating autobiographical novel about his experiences called *Machorka, Roman einer Gefangenschaft*. Machorka is the cheap Russian tobacco that was bartered or sold by prisoners or given as a reward by guards, which forms the story's connecting thread. But Douliez, as the main character is called, was lucky.

Although he fell ill at the first place he was housed,

a barracks in Fürstenwalde, Germany, he heard a piano. The Russians love music and in addition to making their POWs work they wanted to offer some agreeable ways of passing the time. So they organized an audition to find a suitable pianist for the instrument. The man in charge of the search was a German actor named Erik Ode, who later starred as Der Kommissar in a popular German television series of the same name. It goes without saying that Douliez, a professional musician, passed the audition. From that moment on he occupied a privileged position, playing recitals and giving piano lessons to the wives of Soviet soldiers. But soon, the prisoners were transported through Frankfurt am Main to the Soviet Union.

Douliez's job remained the same: he looked after the music. In a camp in Kyzyl-Kyya, partly because of his knowledge of foreign languages Douliez became the director of a cultural center of sorts. There, a ragtag bunch of prisoners listened while he conducted the orchestra he had managed to rustle up. For music lovers, it is fascinating to read how he managed to create an orchestra using the limited number of diverse instruments available; the majority were accordions. He had to delve into his memory to write down pieces he knew by heart and arrange them for the instruments at his disposal. But the prisoners had no access to manuscript paper, so they drew musical staves onto rough-textured cement sacks fashioned into paper. The repertoire was broad: classical music, well-known folk songs, even a few Jewish ones. During one of his interrogations, he met the Russian composer Pyotr Schubin, whose songs he had orchestrated for the radio during the prewar era. Douliez eagerly described the arrangements he had made of works by Eisler and Kurt Weill, and his collaborations with Ernst Busch. He almost seemed homesick. Or was it an opportunistic attempt to gain the approval of the Soviet camp leaders? Was Douliez prompted to make another U-turn and become a socialist Nazi? In the novel, a Russian officer asks him how he ended up in a Russian prisoner of war camp. He answers:

> You must understand that there is no easy answer. Look, whenever the Germans occupy Belgium — twice this century alone — countless Flemish people fraternize with their Eastern neighbors. That has nothing to do with that particular moment's political or military situation. It's all about the people: Northern Germans and Flemish people are cut from the same cloth. That's why it doesn't matter if, according to German accounts, the legendary Till Eulenspiegel came from the Braunschweig region and died in 1350 in Lübeck. Or, as described by Belgian novelist Charles de Coster, he came from Damme in Flanders and wreaked havoc on Spanish tyrants two hundred years later. He embodies the timeless trickster and the unity of the Nether-German spirit.

Douliez, meanwhile, had been tried in absentia. He was sentenced to death and ordered to pay damages amounting to five hundred thousand Belgian francs. After he returned to his native land, his sentence was reduced to twelve years, and in 1951 he was released from the prison in Saint-Gillis, Belgium. However, Belgium had banned him from practicing his profession, so he left for Germany to begin a second career in the music world. He conducted the orchestra of the Deutsche Oper Berlin in a recording of Tchaikovsky's *Nutcracker Suite*, released on the celebrated RCA label. He was also the head of a record company in Stuttgart for a time. He wrote books about Peter Benoit, Johann Strauss II, and Claude Debussy, and he put together a collection of art songs and arias. But for those books, he used a pen name, as he did when writing music for *Fräulein Else*, a film based on Arthur Schnitzler's play. The film was produced by the Belgian Radio and Television network in 1970 and directed by Douliez's daughter, Ivonne Lex. Douliez's pseudonym was Paul Kuringer, referring to a borough in Hasselt where he was born. And so, under an assumed name, he was able to walk into the old Flagey Building with music for a play by a Jewish writer. Can that really be considered *Wiedergutmachung*, or making amends?

Aronson, Josh, dir. *Orchestra of Exiles*. Aronson Film Associates, United Channel Movies. http://www.aronsonfilms.com /orchestra-of-exiles.html.

Aronson, Peter. *Bronislaw Huberman: From Child Prodigy to Hero, the Violinist Who Saved Jewish Musicians from the Holocaust.* New York: Double M Books, 2018.

Bade, Patrick. *Music Wars, 1937–1945*. London: East and West Publishing, 2012.

Boehmer, Konrad and Jacq Firmin Vogelaar. *Hanns Eisler: Muziek en politiek*. Nijmegen: SUN, 1972.

Bor, J. *Theresienstädter requiem: Novelle*. Berlin: Buchverlag der Morgen, 1975.

Bor, Josef, et al. *The Terezin Requiem*. New York: Avon Books, 1978.

Bosveld, Johan. *Componist Van Hitler: Franz Lehár, Operette en Ontkenning in Wenen*. Utrecht: Uitgeverij het Spectrum, 2013.

Bredschneyder, Fred. *Ik Hou Van Holland: Een Levensbeeld Van Joseph Schmidt in Feiten, Gebeurtenissen en Herinneringen*. Nieuwkoop: Heuff,1981.

"Bronislaw Huberman." http://bronislawhuberman.com [no longer valid].

Craft, Robert. "Jews and Geniuses." *New York Review*, 16 February 1989.

Davidson, Susie, et al. *The Music Man of Terezin: The Story of Rafael Schaechter as Remembered by Edgar Krasa*. Somerville, MA: Ibbetson Street Press, 2012.

Denscher, Barbara, and Helmut Peschina. *Kein Land des Lächelns Fritz Löhner-Beda, 1883–1942*. Frankfurt/Main: Residenz-Verl, 2000.

Douliez, Paul. *Machorka: Roman einer Gefangenschaft*. Munich: Ehrenwirth Verlag, 1979.

Egk, Werner. *Die Zeit wartet nicht*. Mainz: Schott, 2001.

Eisler, Hanns. "Statements by Hanns Eisler under Interrogation by the House Committee on Un-American Activities and about His Deportation from the USA." https://tagg.org/others/eisler/statements.html.

Encyclopedia of Genocide and Crimes against Humanity. Encyclopedia.com. https://www.encyclopedia.com /international/encyclopedias-almanacs-transcripts -and-maps/music-theresienstadt.

Fassbind, Alfred A. *Joseph Schmidt: Sein Lied ging um die Welt*. Zurich: Römerhof Verlag, 2012.

Frey, Stefan. *Was sagt ihr zu diesem Erfolg: Franz Lehár und die Unterhaltungsmusik des 20. Jahrhunderts*. Frankfurt am Main: Insel Verlag, 1995.

Goebbels, Joseph, and Fröhlich Elke. *Die tagebücher von Joseph Goebbels*. Munich: K.G. Saur Verlag, 1998.

Griffiths, Paul. *Modern Music: A Concise History: 134 Illustrations*. London: Thames and Hudson, 1996.

Griffiths, Paul. *Olivier Messiaen and the Music of Time*. London: Faber, 2012.

Grun, Bernard. *Gold und Silber; Franz Lehár und seine Welt*. Munich: Langen-Müller, 1970.

Hartmann, Rudolf. *Richard Strauss: Die Bühnenwerke von der Uraufführung bis Heute*. Munich: Piper Verlag, 1980.

Hennenberg, Fritz. *Hanns Eisler*. Hamburg: Rowohlt Verlag, 1987.

Hindemith, Paul, et al. *"Das private Logbuch": Briefe an seine Frau Gertrud*. Munich: Piper Verlag, 1995.

Homepage—Stiftung gedenkstätten Buchenwald und Mittelbau-Dora. http://www.buchenwald.de.

"The Huberman Violin—UC Santa Barbara Arts & Lectures." https://houstonsymphony.org/the-huberman-violin -by-joshua-bell/.

Jonke, Gert, et al. *La Mort d'Anton Webern: En un clin d'oeil aveugle: Récit*. Rieux en Val, France: Verdier, 2000.

Karas Joža. *Music in Terezin, 1941–1945*. New York: Beaufort Books, 1985.

Kater, M. H. *Composers of the Nazi Era: Eight Portraits*. New York: Oxford University Press, 1997.

Lasker-Wallfisch, Anita. *Inherit the Truth, 1939–1945: The Documented Experiences of a Survivor of Auschwitz and Belsen*. London: Giles de la Mare, 1996.

Lebrecht, Norman. *The Maestro Myth: Great Conductors in Pursuit of Power*. London: Simon and Schuster, 1991.

Lebrecht, Norman. *When the Music Stops: Managers, Maestros and the Corporate Murder of Classical Music.* London: Simon and Schuster, 1999.

McMullen, John William. *The Miracle of Stalag 8A: Beauty beyond the Horror: Olivier Messiaen and the Quatuor pour la fin du temps, "Quartet for the End of Time."* Evansville, IN: Bird Brain, 2010.

Messiaen, Pierre. *Images.* Paris: Desclée, De Brouwer, 1944.

Metz Günther. *Der Fall Hindemith: Versuch einer Neubewertung.* Frankfurt am Main: Wolke Verlag, 2016.

Mittelbau-Dora, Stiftung Gedenkstätte Buchenwald und. "Für Besuch der ausstellungen Gilt die '2g-Regel.'" Homepage— Stiftung gedenkstätten Buchenwald und Mittelbau-Dora.

Moldenhauer, Hans. *The Death of Anton Webern: A Drama in Documents.* Whitefish, MT: Literary Licensing, 2011.

Music. https://holocaustmusic.ort.org/music.

The National Archives. "The Discovery Service." *Discovery.* The National Archives, 12 August 2009. https://discovery.nationalarchives.gov.uk.

"The Orel Foundation: Rediscovering Suppressed Musical Treasures of the Twentieth Century." http://orelfoundation.org.

Osborne, Richard. *Herbert von Karajan: A Life in Music.* Missoula, MT: Pimlico, 2014.

Paul Abraham: Der tragische König der Jazz-Operette. https://paul-abraham-bio.de.

"Paul Hindemith: Aktuelles." *Startseite: Paul Hindemith.* http://www.hindemith.info.

Prieberg, Fred K. *Musik im NS-Staat.* Frankfurt am Main: Fischer Taschenbuch, 2015.

Prokofiev, Sergey Sergeevich, and Anthony Phillips. *Diaries.* London: Faber, 2012.

"Die Prozesse gegen Industrielle / IG Farben." *Deutschlandfunk Kultur.* https://www.deutschlandfunkkultur.de/die-prozesse-gegen-industrielle-ig-farben-100.html.

Rathkolb, Oliver. *Führertreu und Gottbegnadet: Künstlereliten im Dritten Reich.* Vienna: Österreichischer Bundesverlag, 1991.

Riehle, Klaus. *Herbert von Karajan—Die wahrheit Während und nach Hitler eine Aufarbeitung.* Vienna: Ibera Verlag–European University Press Verlagsgesellschaft M.b.H, 2016.

Robijns, J., et al. *Algemene Muziek Encyclopedie.* Haarlem: De Haan, 1979.

Ross, Alex. *The Rest Is Noise: Listening to the Twentieth Century.* New York: Fourth Estate, 2012.

Sachs, Harvey. *Music in Fascist Italy.* New York: Weidenfeld and Nicolson, 1987.

Schaller, Wolfgang. *Operette unterm Hakenkreuz zwischen hoffähiger Kunst und "Entartung": Beiträge einer Tagung der Staatsoperette Dresden.* Berlin: Metropol Verlag, 2007.

Schwarberg Günther. *Dein ist mein ganzes Herz: Die Geschichte von Fritz Löhner-Beda, der die schönsten Lieder der Welt Schrieb, und warum Hitler ihn ermorden ließ.* Göttingen, Germany: Steidl, 2000.

Siohan, Robert. *Stravinsky.* Paris: Editions du Seuil, 1982.

Stolz, Robert, et al. *Die ganze Welt ist Himmelblau.* Cologne: Bastei Lübbe, Bergisch Gladbach, 1986.

Stravinsky, Igor, and Robert Craft. *Stravinsky Selected Correspondence.* New York: Knopf, 1981.

Szalsza, Piotr. *Bronisław Huberman: Leben und Leidenschaften eines vergessenen Genies.* Vienna: Hollitzer Verlag, 2019.

Taruskin, Richard. *The Danger of Music and Other Anti-utopian Essays.* Berkeley: University of California Press, 2010.

Taruskin, Richard. *Defining Russia Musically: Historical and Hermeneutical Essays.* Princeton, NJ: Princeton University Press, 1997.

Taruskin, Richard. *Stravinsky and the Russian Tradition: A Biography of the Works through Marva.* Berkeley: University of California Press, 1996.

"Terezin Music Foundation." http://www.terezinmusic.org.

"Theater Aachen." https://theateraachen.de/de_DE/home.

"Tutzings Historie." *Gemeinde Tutzing,* 15 June 2021. http://www.tutzing.de/tutzings-historie.

United States Holocaust Memorial Museum. "Music of the Holocaust." https://www.ushmm.org/collections/the -museums-collections/collections-highlights/music-of -the-holocaust-highlights-from-the-collection/music-of -the-holocaust.

Von Dieter David Scholz. "Neues Buch über Karajan — Kein Nazi, aber ein opportunistischer Mitläufer." *Deutschland-funk.* https://www.deutschlandfunk.de/neues-buch-ueber -karajan-kein-nazi-aber-ein-100.html.

Waller, Klaus. *Paul Abraham—Der tragische König der Operette: Eine Biographie*. Hamburg: Books on Demand, 2017.

Youngkin, Stephen D. *The Lost One: A Life of Peter Lorre*. Lexington: University Press of Kentucky, 2012.

Zweig, Stefan. *Die Welt von Gestern*. Cologne: Anaconda Verlag, 2013.

TRANSLATOR'S SOURCES

"Anton Webern." *Wikipedia*, Wikimedia Foundation. https://
en.wikipedia.org/wiki/Anton_Webern.

"Einheitsfrontlied." *Wikipedia*, Wikimedia Foundation. https://
en.wikipedia.org/wiki/Einheitsfrontlied.

Gellately, Robert. *The Oxford Illustrated History of the Third Reich*.
New York: Oxford University Press, 2018.

Geocaching. "Gedenkstätten Teil 11—Der blonde Hans."
Geocaching. https://www.geocaching.com/geocache
/GC44B3G_gedenkstatten-teil-11-der-blonde-hans.

"Huberman in Recital." *Arbiter of Cultural Traditions*.
https://arbiterrecords.org/catalog/huberman-in-recital.

"Igor Stravinsky." *Wikipedia*, Wikimedia Foundation.
https://en.wikipedia.org/wiki/Igor_Stravinsky.

"The Most Powerful Man in Classical Music." *Spectator Australia*.
https://www.spectator.com.au/2015/06/the-most-powerful
-man-in-classical-music.

"Quatuor pour la fin du temps." *Wikipedia*, Wikimedia
Foundation, 14 July 2021. https://en.wikipedia.org/wiki
/Quatuor_pour_la_fin_du_temps.

"Quotes by Bronislaw Huberman: A-Z Quotes." https://
www.azquotes.com/author/35566-Bronislaw_Huberman.
"Stravinsky and Fascism (Corrected!)" Narkive: Newsgroup
Archive. https://rec.music.classical.recordings.narkive.com
/wqzy34z4/stravinsky-and-fascism-corrected.

1. "Ja so ein Mädel, ungarisches Mädel." From *Victoria and Her Hussar.* Composed by Paul Abraham. Performed by Peter Alexander.

2. "Reich mir zum Abschied noch einmal die Hände." From *Victoria and Her Hussar.* Composed by Paul Abraham. Performed by Rudolf Schock and Margit Schramm.

3. "Toujours l'amour." From *Ball at the Savoy.* Composed by Paul Abraham. Performed by Erika Köth. Conducted by August Peter Waldenmaier with the Vienna Festspielhaus Orchestra.

4. "Pardon Madame." From *Victoria and Her Hussar.* Composed by Paul Abraham. Performed by Richard Tauber.

5. "Yokohama Mama." From *Victoria and Her Hussar.* Composed by Paul Abraham. Performed by Lizzi Waldmüller and Oszkár Dénes.

6. Lied aus "Der Gatte des Fräuleins." Composed by Paul Abraham. (In Hungarian.) Performed by Róbert Rátonyi.

7. "Bin kein Hauptmann, bin kein Offizier." Composed by Paul Abraham. Performed by the Comedian Harmonists.

8. *Victoria and Her Hussar.* Composed by Paul Abraham. (Filmed version of the operette.)

9. *The Force of Destiny* (overture). Composed by Giuseppe Verdi. Performed by Arturo Toscanini.

10. Symphony no. 9, op. 125. Composed by Ludwig van Beethoven. Conducted by Arturo Toscanini.

11. Rehearsal of Johannes Brahms' Symphony no. 2, Arturo Toscanini in a rage.

12. *Tannhäuser* (overture). Composed by Richard Wagner. Conducted by Arturo Toscanini with the NBC Symphony Orchestra.

13. Symphony no. 5 in C Minor, op. 67: 1. Allegro con brio. Composed by Ludwig van Beethoven. Conducted by Arturo Toscanini with the NBC Symphony Orchestra.

14. "The Hymn of the Nations." Composed by Giuseppe Verdi. Conducted by Arturo Toscanini with the NBC Symphony Orchestra.

15. *Thus Spoke Zarathustra.* Composed by Richard Strauss. Conducted by Mariss Jansons with the Royal Concertgebouw Orchestra.

16. *Die schweigsame Frau*, op. 80, Potpourri (overture). Composed by Richard Strauss. Conducted by Marek Janowski with the Staatskapelle Dresden.

17. "Wie schön ist doch die Musik." From *Die schweigsame Frau*, op. 80, TrV. 265, act 3. Composed by Richard Strauss. Performed by Thomas Quasthoff with the Orchester der Deutschen Oper Berlin.

18. *The Silent Woman.* Composed by Richard Strauss. Conducted by Wolfgang Sawallisch with the Choir and Orchestra of the Bavarian State Opera.

19. "Silentium! Herrn Schneidebart." From *The Silent Woman*. Composed by Richard Strauss. Conducted by Pedro Halffter with the Choir and Orchestra of the Bavarian State Opera.

20. "Metamorphosen." Composed by Richard Strauss. Conducted by Mariss Jansons with the Royal Concertgebouw Orchestra.

21. *The Silent Woman*, act 3. Composed by Richard Strauss. Conducted by Wolfgang Sawallisch with the Bavarian State Orchestra.

22. Oboe Concerto in D Major. Composed by Richard Strauss. Performed by François Leleux with the Aurora Orchestra.

23. "Four Last Songs." Composed by Richard Strauss. Performed by Jessye Norman with the Orchestre de la Suisse Romande.

24. Piano Sonata no. 14 in C-sharp Minor, op. 27, no. 2, "Moonlight": 1. Adagio sostenuto. Composed by Ludwig van Beethoven. Performed by Elly Ney.

25. Piano Concerto no. 3, op. 37, and Piano Concerto no. 4, op. 58. Composed by Ludwig van Beethoven. Performed by Elly Ney and Willem van Hoogstraten with the Nuremberg Symphony Orchestra.

26. Piano Concerto no. 5 in E-flat Major, op. 73. Composed by Ludwig van Beethoven. Conducted by Karl Böhm. Performed by Elly Ney with the Vienna Philharmonic.

27. "Messa da Requiem." Composed by Giuseppe Verdi. Conducted by Andrés Orozco-Estrada with the Frankfurt Radio Symphony.

28. *Pulcinella* (suite). Composed by Igor Stravinsky. Conducted by Alondra de la Parra with the Tonhalle Orchester Zürich.

29. *Petrushka*. Composed by Igor Stravinsky. Conducted by Andrís Nelsons with the Royal Concertgebouw Orchestra.

30. *Der Rosenkavalier* (suite). Composed by Richard Strauss. Conducted by Yannick Nézet-Séguin with the Bavarian Radio Symphony Orchestra.

31. "Minuetto and Finale." From *Pulcinella*. Composed by Igor Stravinsky. Conducted by Igor Stravinsky with the Toronto Symphony.

32. *Pulcinella*. Composed by Igor Stravinsky. Performed by Claudio Abbado with the London Symphony Orchestra.

33. "Duo Concertant." Composed by Igor Stravinsky. Performed by Itzhak Perlman and Bruno Canino.

34. *Petrushka.* Composed by Igor Stravinsky. Conducted by Andrei Chistyakov with the Bolshoi Theatre Academic State Orchestra.

35. Duo Concertante for Piano and Violin. Composed by Igor Stravinsky. Performed by Peter Laul and Ilya Gringolts.

36. Concerto for Two Pianos. Composed by Igor Stravinsky. Performed by Lucas Jussen and Arthur Jussen.

37. *Symphony of Psalms.* Composed by Igor Stravinsky. Conducted by Sir Georg Solti with the Chicago Symphony Orchestra.

38. "Sarasate Nocturne," op. 9, no. 2, by Frédéric Chopin, and "Auer Musical Moment," no. 3, by Franz Schubert. Performed by Bronisław Huberman.

39. Violin Concerto in D Major, op. 77. Composed by Johannes Brahms. Performed by Bronisław Huberman.

40. *Passacaglia,* op. 1. Composed by Anton Webern. Performed by Pierre Boulez with the London Symphony Orchestra.

41. *Im Sommerwind.* Composed by Anton Webern. Conducted by Christoph von Dohnányi with the Cleveland Orchestra.

42. "Musical Offering, BWV 1079 — no. 2 Ricercar a 6." Composed by Johann Sebastian Bach, arranged by Anton Webern. Conducted by Paavo Järvi with the Berliner Philharmoniker.

43. "Quartet for the End of Time." Composed by Olivier Messiaen. Performed by the Het Collectief.

44. "Poèmes pour Mi." Composed by Olivier Messiaen. Performed by María Orán and Yvonne Loriod.

45. "Träumerei." Composed by Robert Schumann. Performed by Raphael Wallfisch.

46. "Marche militaire." Composed by Franz Schubert. Performed by the Boston Cello Quartet.

47. "Träumerei." From *Kinderszenen*, op. 15. Composed by Robert Schumann. Performed by Mischa Maisky.

48. "Playing for Time." From *Auschwitz*. Composed by Arthur Miller. Performer uncredited.

49. *Suite "1922,"* op. 26. Composed by Paul Hindemith. Performed by Esther Walker.

50. Octet; I. Adagio. Allegro con brio. Composed by Paul Hindemith. Performed by the Brooklyn Chamber Music Society.

51. Octet; III. Langsam. Composed by Paul Hindemith. Performed by the Brooklyn Chamber Music Society.

52. Octet; V. Fuge. Composed by Paul Hindemith. Performed by the Brooklyn Chamber Music Society.

53. *Mathis der Maler*. Composed by Paul Hindemith. Conducted by Herbert Blomstedt with the Gustav Mahler Jugendorchester.

54. "Buchenwald-Lied." Composed by Hermann Leopoldi, lyrics by Fritz Löhner-Beda. Performed by Ernst Busch.

55. "Du schwarzer Zigeuner." Composed by Karel Vacek, lyrics by Fritz Löhner-Beda. Performed by Vico Torriani.

56. "Ich hab' mein Herz in Heidelberg verloren." Composed by Fred Raymond, lyrics by Fritz Löhner-Beda and Ernst Neubach. Performed by Hermann Prey.

57. "Das alte Lied." Composed by Henry Love, lyrics by Fritz Löhner-Beda. Performed by Rudolf Schock.

58. "Dein ist mein ganzes Herz." Composed by Franz Lehár. Performed by Fritz Wunderlich.

59. "Oh, Donna Clara." Composed by Fritz Löhner-Beda and Jerzy Petersburski. Performed by Annette Postel with the SalonOrchester Schwanen.

60. "Freunde, das Leben ist lebenswert." From *Giuditta*. Composed by Frans Lehár, lyrics by Fritz Löhner-Beda. Conducted by Emmerich Smola with the SWR Rundfunkorchester Kaiserslautern.

61. "Meine Lippen, sie küssen so heiss." From *Giuditta*. Composed by Franz Lehár, lyrics by Fritz Löhner-Beda. Conducted by David Charles Abell. Performed by Diana Damrau with the Royal Liverpool Philharmonic Orchestra.

62. Symphony no. 3 in E-flat Major, op. 55, *Eroica*. Composed by Ludwig van Beethoven. Conducted by Willem Mengelberg with the New York Philharmonic Orchestra.

63. Symphony no. 2, *Auferstehung*. Composed by Gustav

Mahler. Conducted by Mariss Jansons with the Netherlands Radio Choir.

64. *Die lustige Witwe* (*The Merry Widow*). Composed by Franz
Lehár. Conducted by Herbert von Karajan.

65. "Heut' ist der schönste Tag in meinem Leben." Composed
by Hans May. Performed by Joseph Schmidt.

66. "Du sollst der Kaiser meiner Seele sein." Composed by
Robert Stolz. Performed by Joseph Schmidt.

67. "I'll Sing a Song of Love to You." Composed by Hans
May. Performed by Joseph Schmidt.

68. "Ja, das alles auf Ehr." Composed by Johann Strauss II.
Performed by Joseph Schmidt.

69. "A Star Falls from Heaven." Composed by Hans May.
Performed by Joseph Schmidt.

70. "Ach, so fromm." Composed by Friedrich von Flotow.
Performed by Joseph Schmidt.

71. "E lucevan le stelle." From *Tosca*. Composed by Giacomo
Puccini. Performed by Joseph Schmidt.

72. "Recondita armonia." From *Tosca*. Composed by
Giacomo Puccini. Performed by Joseph Schmidt.

73. "Non piangere, Liù." From *Turandot*. Composed by
Giacomo Puccini. Performed by Joseph Schmidt.

74. "Nessun dorma." From *Turandot*. Composed by Giacomo
Puccini. Performed by Joseph Schmidt.

75. Piano Concerto no. 23 in A Major, K. 488. Composed
by Wolfgang Amadeus Mozart. Conducted by Adrian

Boult. Performed by Myra Hess with the London Philharmonic Orchestra.

76. "Jesu, Joy of Man's Desiring." Composed by Johann Sebastian Bach. Performed by Myra Hess.

77. Piano Concerto no. 3 in C Minor. Composed by Ludwig van Beethoven. Conducted by Arturo Toscanini. Performed by Myra Hess.

78. "Inno delle nazioni." Composed by Giuseppe Verdi. Conducted by Arturo Toscanini. Performed by Jan Peerce with the Westminster Choir and the NBC Symphony Orchestra.

79. "The Star Spangled Banner." Harmonized and orchestrated by Igor Stravinsky. Conducted by Michael Tilson Thomas with the London Symphony Orchestra.

80. String Quartet no. 62, op. 76, no. 3, *Emperor*. Composed by Joseph Haydn. Performed by the Veridis Quartet.

81. Symphony no. 7, *Leningrad*. Composed by Dmitri Shostakovich. Conducted by Marin Alsop with the Frankfurt Radio Symphony Orchestra.

82. *Water Music*. Composed by George Frideric Handel. Performed by Georg Kallweit with the Akademie für Alte Musik Berlin.

83. "Ein feste Burg ist unser Gott," BWV 80. Composed by Johann Sebastian Bach. Conducted by John Eliot Gardiner with the Monteverdi Choir and the English Baroque Soloists.

84. *Kol Nidrei.* Composed by Max Bruch. Conducted by Paavo Järvi. Performed by Mischa Maisky with the Frankfurt Radio Symphony.
85. *Die Meistersinger von Nürnberg* (overture). Composed by Richard Wagner. Conducted by Christian Thielemann with the Philadelphia Orchestra.
86. "Fanfare for the Common Man." Composed by Aaron Copland and John Ryan. Performed by the National Symphony Orchestra.
87. "The White Cliffs of Dover," Composed by Walter Kent and Nat Burton, and "We'll Meet Again," Composed by Ross Parker and Hughie Charles. Performed by Dame Vera Lynn.
88. "When the Lights Go On Again (All Over the World)." Composed by Bennie Benjamin, Sol Marcus, and Eddie Seiler. Performed by Dame Vera Lynn.
89. "Beneath the Lights of Home." Composed by Walter Jurmann and Bernie Grossman. Performed by Deanna Durbin.
90. "Ich weiss, es wird einmal ein Wunder geschehen." Composed by Bruno Balz and Michael Jary. Performed by Zarah Leander.
91. "Lili Marleen." Composed by Norbert Schultze and Hans Leip. Performed by Lale Andersen.
92. "Jeep Jockey Jump." Composed by Jerry Gray. Performed by Glenn Miller.

93. "Einheitsfrontlied" ("United Front Song"). Composed by Bertolt Brecht and Hanns Eisler. Conducted by Dietrich Knothe with the Berliner Singakademie.

94. "Solidaritätslied" ("Solidarity Song"). Composed by Hanns Eisler. Conducted by Dietrich Knothe. Performed by HK Gruber with the Rundfunk-Sinfonie-Orchester Berlin and the Rundfunk-Chor Berlin.

95. "Lied von der belebenden Wirkung des Geldes." Composed by Bertolt Brecht and Hanns Eisler. Performed by Gisela May.

96. "Seifenlied." Composed by Hanns Eisler and Kurt Tucholsky. Performed by Ernst Busch.

97. Suite no. 3, "Kuhle Wampe." Composed by Hans Eisler. Conducted by Heinz Rögner. Performed by the Rundfunk-Simfonie-Orchester Berlin.

98. *Niemandsland* (suite), no. 2, op. 24: II. Capriccio über jüdische Volkslieder. Composed by Hanns Eisler. Conducted by Heinz Rögner with the Rundfunk-Sinfonie-Orchester Berlin.

99. "An eine Stadt" (Hölderlin-Fragmente). From *The Hollywood Songbook*. Composed by Hanns Eisler. Performed by Matthias Goerne and Eric Schneider.

100. Polonaise in A-flat Major, op. 53, "Heroic." Composed by Frédéric Chopin. Performed by Paul Douliez.

101. "Am Rio Jarama." From *On the Jarama Front*. Composed by Ernst Busch and David Martin. Performed by Paul Douliez.

102. "Tanz der Stunden." Composed by Amilcare Ponchielli. Performed by Paul Douliez with the Orchester der Staatsoper Berlin.

To access the *Beethoven in the Bunker* YouTube playlist, visit http://www.otherpress.com/beethoven

If accessed from the United States, the playlist includes 102 entries. Additional entries (up to 109) may appear in this playlist if accessed from outside the United States.

PHOTO CREDITS